Thomas Bowman

Historical Review Of The Disturbance in the Evangelical Association

Thomas Bowman

Historical Review Of The Disturbance in the Evangelical Association

ISBN/EAN: 9783743354982

Manufactured in Europe, USA, Canada, Australia, Japa

Cover: Foto ©ninafisch / pixelio.de

Manufactured and distributed by brebook publishing software (www.brebook.com)

Thomas Bowman

Historical Review Of The Disturbance in the Evangelical Association

Historical Review

—BY—

BISHOP BOWMAN.

Historical Review

—OF THE—

Disturbance in the Evangelical Association.

By BISHOP THOMAS BOWMAN.

Published by authority of the BOARD OF PUBLICATION,

—AND—

Approved by the BOARD OF BISHOPS.

CLEVELAND, OHIO,
Published by *THOMAS & MATTILL*,
1894.

Preface.

The Board of Publication, at its session in October, 1892, passed a resolution requesting the Board of Bishops to compile a brief history of the late disturbance in our beloved Church. At a subsequent meeting of the bishops, the undersigned was appointed to prepare the work for the press.

The one great difficulty I encountered was the lack of time needed in its preparation, as the calls for episcopal work were very pressing from all sides, especially as four of the conferences under the special supervision of our senior Bishop were assigned to me during his visit to the Sun Rise Kingdom, to organize the first Annual Conference of our Church in Heathen lands, Bishop Horn being in Europe and Bishop Breyfogle on the Pacific Coast on official duty. Hence only such hours could be devoted to this special work as were not absolutely needed in the performance of the general duties of my office.

After the work was finally completed it was carefully read and examined by my worthy colleagues, and by them approved, so that this historical sketch of the great revolt against the authority, and even the very life of our Church is "in every sense of the word" an official statement of the commencement, development and end of a most gigantic conspiracy.

It was the purpose of the Board of Publication to have the work condensed into as small a compass as possible, in order that it might be placed in the hands of our people at small cost, hence I was compelled to group together the vast material at hand, into as small proportions as could be and yet make myself understood.

I offer no apology for presenting the true inwardness of this stupendous crime against religion, and ecclesiastical order, described in these pages, in plain language. The rebellion, the history of which is sketched in this unpretentious volume, was so utterly unjustifiable, and was inaugurated and carried on in such a spirit of malicousness and personal animosity against the officials of the Church in assailing their personal and official character, publicly and privately, that the circumstances not only justified but demanded at least, plain, if not vigorous language.

The evidence for the statements made in this work is in our possession. Every statement made can be verified either by living witnesses or documentary evidence, whenever it may become necessary to do so.

The purpose of this volume is to bring out and present in permanent form, the main facts connected with this disturbance in order to enable the reader as well as the future historian of the Church, to become acquainted with its inner history as well as its outward developments. Moreover, it is hoped that many of those who have been led away and deceived by ministers who were unfaithful to their solemn vows will read these pages, and be led to see the error of their way, and resolve to remain with the Church which under God has been instrumental in their salvation. Why leave this church and aid in organizing a new sect in this age of the world? It has done them no violence,— they have at no time felt any "yoke" when they were acting in accord with the laws of our dear Church, save the easy yoke of our blessed Redeemer. God is richly blessing the Evangelical Association. Why not remain and share these blessings and worship God in the Church buildings they have helped to erect?

The regulations of our Church are not only in accordance with the Word of God, but they are the result of experience, and have been framed by men of God. In all cases they have been adopted by the majority of those who were duly elected to represent the Church, even by a majority of three-fourths in the General Conference, and two-thirds by the ministers of the Church, assembled in Annual Conference sessions, and all have obligated themselves to defend and obey these regulations. Certainly in all republican forms of government majorities must rule, or else disorder and revolution will result, and when anarchy with its spirit of destruction is asserting itself in nearly all lands, Christians should set an example of obedience to law and order.

I am indebted to Rev. M. Pfitzinger of the New York Conference, who was for a series of years the secretary of the Board of Trustees of North Western College, located at Naperville, Ill., and is the president of the board at this time, for much valuable information respecting the history of that institution. Also to Rev. C. C. Pfund, for furnishing me with the facts connected with the attempts in the Iowa Conference to seize upon the property of the Church, and also to Rev. H. E. Linse of the Minnesota Conference, for the facts connected with the bold attempt to steal our valuable Church property in St. Paul, Minn.

I would have greatly preferred to have either of my worthy colleagues prepare this work for the press; still, I felt it to be my duty to comply with their wishes, and trust that it may be the means of leading many out of darkness into light.

Chicago, Oct. 10, 1893.   THOMAS BOWMAN.

CONTENTS.

Introduction IX

CHAPTER I.
The Origin of the Church and the First Signs of Disloyalty. 1

CHAPTER II.
Rudolph Dubs is Elected Bishop in Order " to Put Esher Down," and the Results Following........................ 18

CHAPTER III.
The Ecumenical Conference Affair................................ 44

CHAPTER IV.
Clewell for Assistant Editor of the *Messenger* 53

CHAPTER V.
Efforts Looking Towards an Amicable Adjustment of the Difficulties.. 61

CHAPTER VI.
The Difficulties Connected with Our Mission in Japan 80

CHAPTER VII.
The General Conference of 1887, and What Soon Followed 97

CHAPTER VIII.
The Trial and Conviction of Bishop Dubs...................... 121

CHAPTER IX.
The Attempt to Disorganize the Church 127

CHAPTER X.

Attempts to Alienate Church Property in the Interests of the Rebellion...... 155

CHAPTER XI.

The Harvest...... 184

CHAPTER XII.

The Situation at Present and the Outlook for the Future... 195

Introduction.

BY BISHOP J. J. ESHER.

(Translated from the German by Bishop S. C. Breyfogel.)

From the beginning the history of the Kingdom of God on earth has been a record of suffering and of conflict, within and without. Christ, our Lord, the great Head of the Church, Himself had to pass through suffering into His glory and through a hard-won victory, to ascend the throne of His sovereignty. And in like manner, as He became perfect through suffering, and through conflict gained His complete victory, so His Church has endured through all her conflicts, been preserved in all her sufferings, and been purified like as refined gold.

This experience of the Church universal, and of every part thereof has also repeated itself in the history of the Evangelical Association, from her origin until this very hour. At first it was hatred from without only, however, not from the Jews, and Gentiles, but from professed Christians seeking her destruction, but which injured her as little as did the persecutions of old impair, the early Christian Church. Later on, when the Association had compelled recognition, and become correspondingly strengthened without them, as in the days of the primitive Church, internal disturbances arose. Both in the early Christian Church and in the Evangelical Association these disturbing elements were of a similar nature. In both instances all kinds and classes of men were gathered in, some of whom were corrupt, and therefore impure and pernicious, and who proved themselves a foreign and disturbing element in the Church. In both instances, too, there were such as in the beginning were well furnished in the grace of God, and who "did run well," but they subsequently fell from grace, and although they had begun in the Spirit, departed from the simplicity in Christ, ending their course in the flesh, having walked according to the lusts thereof. In the case of the Evangelical Association the Church itself is largely to blame for the disturbance which has arisen, partly because of a benumbing of her divine life, both in its inner and outer manifestations, and partly because of a relaxation of Church Discipline resultant from this. That there were no serious disturbances during the early days of the Evangelical Association is due partly to the pressure of opposition from without, but much more to the power of vital godliness which dwelt within, and to the faithful—though in some instances too rigorous—application of Discipline. The elements favorable to such disturbance, were then already to a greater or less degree at hand. With a decrease of the divine life, and a relaxation of Discipline, all that was yet needed was the presence of competent and willing personal instruments not lacking in selfishness of purpose, assiduous zeal, and sufficient moral elasticity to unite these diverse and unorganized evil elements, not indeed into a unit among themselves, but for a common work of mischief. These instruments of evil were readily found, in fact were themselves lying in wait for a favorable opportunity, which they seized with an eagerness allowing of no further reflection as to whether there was any good or sufficient ground upon which to place themselves in their insurrection against the Church, whether their methods and course of conduct were wise or foolish, whether adapted to the purpose or ill advised. The question of moral right could not in the nature of things, enter into their plans, inasmuch as their project itself lacked altogether every element of moral justification. In fact, they were obliged to renounce all moral obligations before they could resolve upon their course of destruction. And if from the beginning up to the present time, every other historical disturbance in the Christian Church, and the several branches thereof has had its principles for which it contended, whether justifiable or unjustifiable, and its designated causes, it is nevertheless true that this destructive movement in the Evangelical Association is utterly without principle and without the remotest justifying cause, whether real or apparent. No amendment of doctrine, no moral reform, no improvement of church methods, no extension of church operations, no increased support of church institutions was ever contemplated by this agitation. Its only purpose was to overthrow and to destroy, to cause offense, and to bring reproach upon the name and cause of Christ. This is its essence, work and sequence. According to the declarations of the leaders themselves, it was the arbitrary power of one individual man, under which they were no longer willing to suffer and languish, no longer willing to be oppressed, and against which they arose in the spirit of liberty and entered the lists in defence of their dignity and their rights! A more absurd and dishonorable pretext for their movement, they could not have devised, a stronger testimony to its illegality and utter lack of principle, in short to their sacreligious contempt for the rights of the sanctuary, the congregation and the cause of our God, they could not have given.

By their very assumptions, and by the various other reasons which they assign for their course, they themselves, however, directly brand as a falsehood, their statement that they have risen against the tyranny and power of one man. They arrogate to themselves and their party the highest pre-eminent intelligence of the Church, and assert that in numerical strength, they are almost equal to the Church itself, which they designate as "the majority." And yet, notwithstanding this, they cut loose from the institutions of the Church, from its treasuries and from its administration, they hold a separate General Conference, they not only withdraw their support from all the institutions of the Church, but strenuously seek to injure them; they appeal at great costs to the civil tribunals, from which they retire again and again with heavy loss, and all this on account of one man! The pretext becomes the more absurd and insincere in the face of the excellent governmental arrangement of our Church, whereby a bad and despotic man can be easily removed, that is deposed from his office and deprived of his "despotic power." No, the pretence is too absurd and too palpably untrue. The fig leaf doesn't cover. The apron is too transparent. Ordinary prudence should have invented something else. But then what can be said in justification or defense of a cause which, from its very incipiency has been as foolish as it has been wholly wicked. They should have been honest and said, "We are not willing to remain longer under the Disciplinary yoke of the Evangelical Association, and therefore we declare our independence and go our way." A sense of honor and of genuine honesty, if these traits had been present, would necessarily have dictated such a course, and if they had believed themselves entitled to a portion of the possessions, they might have said in addition, "Give me the portion of goods that falleth to me." Instead of this, they assumed the name of the Church, which, by their unfaithfulness, they had smitten in the face, for whose injury and destruction they had labored, and for the alienation of whose property, consecrated to the Lord, they had resorted to every means.

In this wicked agitation there exists a union of two decided antithises,—a total absence of all law, coupled with an unbounded assumption of law and justice. A trampling under foot of things most sacred; associated with the most sanctimonious pretensions, as though by the repeated failures of their evil purposes they had become martyrs deserving of general commiseration, and entitled to public sympathy. It is doubtful whether there ever existed a more grotesquely, pretentious assumption. By a ruthless overriding of all right, this party undertook, through its leaders, to get rid of the bishops of the Church, to secure the control of the institutions and Annual Conferences of the Church, to hold a General Conference without a representation of the Church, and without any right whatever to elect bishops of their own (two of whom had been expelled from the Church in accordance with the provisions of the Discipline,) and to fill the other general offices of the Church; all this in order that, by methods which were in contempt of all right and justice, these party leaders, who had up to this time labored unsuccessfully by means of church politics, to bring the administration of the Church wholly into their hands, hoped to finally gain their end. In the very nature of things, this reckless procedure must needs fail. Such an outcome might have been foreseen even by a blind man. Instead of repenting in sack cloth and ashes before God, of their unreasonable, lawless and unrighteous course, these sorely disappointed leaders, because of the mis-carriage of their schemes, deliver themselves of sanctimonious protestations, and the most dolorous claims to martyrdom. What crooked paths these party leaders followed during the course of years, what methods they adopted, how that nothing was too sacred and nothing too wicked which might answer their purpose, all this Bishop Bowman clearly sets forth in his eminently successful compilation of the facts and occurrences which took place during the progress and development of this revolt. It must be admitted that these men have carried on their work of destruction with a perseverance worthy of a good cause. Aside from this, however, they have conspicuously distinguished themselves by an unbroken succession of foolish and perverse performances. It is but necessary here to recall their attitude toward the bishops of the Church, their violent conduct at a number of Annual Conference sessions, conduct which was a mockery of every sense of right and honor, and above all, the appointment of their own separate General Conference! Had they come to the General Conference at Indianapolis they might possibly have accomplished something. But no, instead of this, in the perversity of their minds, they deprived themselves of their last opportunity and with very unreliable pilots, and without rudder or compass, sailed out upon the turbulent sea. All this is doubtless to be attributed to their evil and radically perverted cause, and to the false spirit which has possessed and actuated them.

But this subject has another side, that of the Church and her divine Helper. Among the many things which might be said here, the following points are presented in this introduction :

1. The Church has never committed a wrong against the disturbers of her peace, has never given them any occasion for their uprising against her life, her institutions, laws and regulations, *never*. In her administration the Church has stood firm by law and order, and in this consists that "despotism" and "tyranny" under which these agitators chafed, and against which they revolted—the inflexible fidelity of the Church to law and order. "*This is the point.*" These disturbers of the peace of our Church were at one time within the Church and under her law and protection, enjoying in common with all others, every privilege of her communion. Genuine fidelity, that fidelity which they solemnly vowed, would have secured to them the real enjoyment of all the privileges and blessings of the Church. It was only because of their unfaithfulness, their departure from God, and their deviation from law and order that they have been brought to their present state.

For this reason the Church is under no obligations to arbitrate with the faithless and those who have became the disturbers of her peace. To speak of "arbitration" is only a further instance of a perverse and unreasonable demand. Nay, the Church has nothing to arbitrate. Standing steadfast and true by her law and order in the future as she has done in the past, she will abide in prosperity.

2. God has graciously aided our Church in her sore struggle. He has done this not only by the immediate influences of His gracious presence, but also by raising such instrumentalities of his help as the circumstances required. It is a significant fact that in our enforced litigation we have not had to fall into

the hands of strangers. In this connection also the General Conference of 1887 is worthy of special mention. How these partisans, with their leaders, exhausted every means to secure the control of that General Conference and the bitter disappointment which followed the miscarriage of their cherished plans is amply set forth by Bishop Bowman. But of certain occurrences at that General Conference he speaks with a personal diffidence which does not permit him to set forth fully and as they actually occurred, matters of the utmost importance. Bishop Dubs as chairman of the conference during the Hartzler trial gave a decision on a point relating to the trial. Instead of giving a brief explanation as is our rule and custom, he made a sophistical so-called argument, not founded upon church law or justice, but based upon foreign and extraneous matter and partly suspended in mid-air by which he sought to frustrate the ends of justice and rule out the investigation. At the conclusion of this long speech by the chairman, Bishop Bowman rose, manifestly moved by the Holy Spirit, and appealed to the conference. He did not reply to Dubs' address, but in calm and simple terms and yet in a striking and impressive manner he submitted his appeal by which he guided the conference to a correct conclusion in this supremely critical and decisive moment. The conference decided against Dubs' ruling. The hand of the Lord helped in a visible manner, by means of His servant Bishop Bowman, and a faithfully minded majority of the conference.

In a similar manner when one of these party leaders rose in the General Conference, and in utter disregard of order and right attempted to read a so-called protest, but which in reality was a denunciation of the General Conference action relative to the Hartzler case, Bishop Bowman, who presided at the time, manifestly endued in a special manner with power from on high, signally overthrew these revolutionary purposes. The might of the Spirit which accompanied the Bishop in this crisis filled the conference with wonder and called forth feelings of devout thanksgiving. It was a memorable and majestic occurrence. It was the hand of the Lord by His servant.

Occurrences of a like character could be related of several Annual Conference sessions where through the decided attitude of Bishop Bowman assisted by divine strength these conferences were recovered from the hands of the destroyers and saved for the Church. Other servants of the Lord in these conferences also co-operated most efficiently to this end.

3. In the remarkable lay movement in Illinois, the wonderful guidance of our God provided an invaluable means of help to rescue from the hands of the destroyer the Illinois Conference, a conference once so flourishing, but subsequently fallen into evil hands, and now again renewed and fruitful, nestling in the very heart of the Church. On this conference the leaders of the revolt had counted much but by means of this uprising of the laymen, the Spirit of the Lord baffled them most effectually. The full significance of this lay movement has not been recognized up to this time, not even by those who took a prominent part in it. It belongs to the special providences in the history of the Evangelical Association and is worthy of a special history.

4. It will be in order also to direct attention to our recent General Conference session. Here laymen from almost every part of the Church gathered in order to unitedly invoke the divine blessing upon the conference, and to strengthen the assembled servants of the Lord. To those who attended that conference the perceptible presence and governing influence of the divine Spirit, will remain an abiding and blessed memory, and it must be evident to all who with an unbiased mind, read the proceedings, how the Lord helped His servants in a special manner with the guidance of the spirit of truth and grace. Never before was a General Conference confronted by such grave problems, and never before did a General Conference meet its obligations more completely. The beneficent hand of God was upon the session in a most conspicuous manner. But never

before, either, did the Church lie prostrate before God in united pleading prayer for a General Conference, as in this instance. The might of united prayer is immeasurable. All this, together with the growing prosperity of the institutions, and general activities of the Evangelical Association, is a proof of the divine favor upon the Church.

5. In our enforced litigation, the living hand of our God is visibly outstretched in behalf of the righteous cause of the Church. Everything points unmistakably to the fact that it is the good pleasure of God to deliver our Church out of her severe conflict and to secure to her future an increasing prosperity.

With the seceders the case is totally different. Their movement, from its very incipiency, and throughout its entire career has been of such a character that the Holy Spirit can have no part in it. It is all the product of another spirit. They cannot speak of ecclesiastical prosperity, for they are no church, neither do they belong to any. Their work is one of destruction, therefore, righteousness and truth cannot dwell with them. Only harm and mischief can result from their operations. All this is clearly set forth in Bishop Bowman's compilation of established facts.

Notwithstanding all this, however, this party arrogate to themselves the right to be recognized as the Evangelical Association, and to usurp and hold the property of the Church wherever they can. Their spokesmen have left no means unemployed to belittle the Church by traducing her overseers, and other servants, and to commend themselves as the personification of persecuted innocence. Through these misrepresentations many otherwise faithful people have been misled and induced to adhere to this party, and, without intending or desiring to do so, are now on the path of the erring.

Besides this, the party leaders by a systematic misrepresentation of facts, and by lying insinuations in the press have earnestly striven to mislead public opinion, to fill the public mind with unworthy suspicions of the Church and to gain for themselves general favor. In this they were not altogether unsuccessful.

All this has at last imperatively demanded a presentation of the true state of affairs, at least up to a certain point. Further concealment would be a sin against the Church, and against the truth itself. Bishop Bowman, at the request of the Board of Bishops of the Church, has rendered the required service. His exposure of the long record of sin on the part of the leaders of the secession was due to the Church, the public, and the cause of truth. And for this exposure neither apology nor commendation is necessary. Truth requires no apology, that which is right, no recommendation.

On the Pacific Ocean, April 14, 1893.

HISTORICAL REVIEW.

CHAPTER I.

The Origin of the Church and the First Signs of Disloyalty.

The Evangelical Association had her origin in Pennsylvania. Her founder and first Bishop, Rev. Jacob Albright, was a Pennsylvanian. Her second Bishop, Rev. John Seybert, was also a Pennsylvanian. Her third Bishop, Rev. Joseph Long, although a resident of Ohio at the time of his election, was a Pennsylvanian by birth.

All the annual conferences of the Association up to 1827, and the first four General Conferences were held in Pennsylvania. All the annual and General Conferences, from 1812 to 1827, were held within the bounds of the Central Pa. Conference.

The first churches of the Association were built in Pennsylvania. The first Book and Printing Establishment was located at New Berlin, Pa. The Charitable Society, as well as the first Missionary Society of the Church was organized in the same State.

The Book and Printing Establishment was officered exclusively by Pennsylvanians, as editors and publishers, until 1847, when Rev. N. Gehr was elected editor of the *Botschafter*. Pennsylvanians, with but one exception, filled the office of Publisher up to 1870, when Rev. W. F. Schneider of the Wisconsin Conference, was elected to that position. The editors of the *Evangelical Messenger* were also with but one exception

Pennsylvanians from the date of its first publication until 1887. The first three corresponding secretaries, and all the treasurers of the Missionary Society of the Association, except for the space of one year, have been Pennsylvanians. During the first half century of the history of the Church the members of the General Conference, with but few exceptions, were Pennsylvanians either by residence or by birth.

As a consequence the entire control and government of the Church practically was in the hands of Pennsylvanians. As the Church began to extend her operations into the great West, and people of other States and nationalities became connected with her organization, this condition of things necessarily inaugurated a change. During this transition period a certain faction arose in Pennsylvania, led by men somewhat narrow in their conceptions in reference to the great command of our Lord, to preach the Gospel to all nations, assiduously cultivated the idea that the Church having had her origin in Pennsylvania, ought, therefore, to be controlled by Pennsylvanians, and that especially persons of foreign birth should be compelled to retire to the rear. The great bulk of the membership and ministry however were eager for the enlargement of her borders, and by no means harbored such a narrow spirit. The above named faction lost no opportunity to cultivate a spirit of opposition to everything which was not in harmony with their contracted and narrow conception. Especially was this the case in the East Pa. Conference. Out of this idea and spirit the "oldest annual conference" theory was born and nurtured until almost every one, not thoroughly acquainted with the history of our Church, was more or less carried away by it.

The fact that a large majority of the general church officers, up to a comparatively recent date, were chosen from Pennsylvania, although the Church has long since outgrown her original Pennsylvania environments, demonstrates very forcibly that she has shown great respect and consideration for that portion of her domain in which she had her origin. Of her ten bishops seven have been from Pennsylvania.

At the General Conference in 1859, Rev. W. W. Orwig, also a Pennsylvanian, was chosen as the colleague of Bishops Seybert and Long. It seems, however, that although he was from the same State, he did not meet with the approval of the "faction" in Pennsylvania. He was too strict a disciplinarian to meet their views, and too firm a believer in, and defender of, the doctrine of entire sanctification, for the leaders of the said faction, who were determined that this doctrine of our Church must be erased or at least greatly modified. At this same General Conference, at which Orwig was elected to the office of Bishop, charges of heresy on the doctrine in question were preferred against Rev. S. Neitz, one of the leading ministers of the East Pa. Conference. The result was a declaration by the General Conference that Neitz's teaching was out of harmony with the doctrine of our Church. In the investigation and trial of these charges, Bishop Orwig had taken a leading part, standing firmly and uncompromisingly for the Church and her doctrines. This course had aroused the ill-feeling and opposition of Neitz, and especially also of his friends in the East Pa. Conference, against the Bishop, so that no opportunity was allowed to pass unemployed to create prejudice against him and against the general management of the Church. Those who were then members of the Church well remember these things. To what extent the opposition against the General Conference and the general church officers had run can be seen in the fact that in 1860, at the session of the East Pa. Conference, immediately following the General Conference of 1859, at which Rev. S. Neitz's teachings were condemned, a resolution prevailed, declaring the conference to be in accord with the minority of the General Conference which had not voted for the resolutions condemning the doctrinal views of Rev. S. Neitz. By this action the East Pa. Conference not only committed itself to the erroneous doctrines of Rev. S. Neitz, but also thus early declared its spirit of opposition to the highest ecclesiastical tribunal of our Church, whose action is final on all subjects.

In 1860, Rev. S. Neitz declared to the compiler of this work, who was then a preacher on trial, that in less than ten years, the chapter defining our doctrine of entire sanctification would be erased from our discipline. This furnishes the key to the purpose of his attacks upon this doctrine in his sermons and writings. And when the action of the Board of Publication in reference to the heresy of Rev. T. G. Clewell, then editor of the *Evangelical Messenger*, on the doctrine of entire sanctification, was acted upon, criticised and condemned, by the East Pa. Conference in Lebanon, Pa., in 1871, it was not done merely on account of personal sympathy for Clewell, nor merely on account of the manner of procedure adopted by the Board, although this was made the pretext for its action; but because the large majority of the conference, then completely controlled by Rev. S. Neitz, was in full sympathy and harmony with the doctrinal views of Clewell, *and demanded liberty* to teach as they believed, without being in any wise restrained by the doctrine of the Church as expressed in her articles of faith and book of discipline. During the discussions, one of the members of the conference, voicing the sentiment of the majority, declared that Clewell's exposition of the doctrine of sanctification had been the clearest, that it was more fully in accord with the teachings of the New Testament, than any utterances which had ever appeared in our church periodicals, and that the *liberty* thus to believe and teach would be defended at all hazards. This action of the East Pa. Conference was declared illegal at the following General Conference and ordered to be expunged from the minutes of that conference. These facts are stated that the reader may see how early the seeds of dissension were sown in the East Pa. Conference, and how under Neitz's leadership it arrogated unto itself a certain censorship over persons and bodies which were not within its jurisdiction.

For the reasons given above it had been determined by the leaders of this Pennsylvania faction that Bishop Orwig must not be re-elected at the expiration of his term. Rev. T. G. Clewell, then editor of the *Evangelical Messenger*, said to Rev. J. J. Esher, then editor of our Sunday School Literature, some time previous to the General Conference of 1863, held in Buffalo, N. Y., that the first bishop, in the history of the Evangelical Association, who would fail to be re-elected, would be Orwig. With this purpose in view, this faction came to Buffalo in 1863, under the leadership of Rev. Solomon Neitz and T. G. Clewell, both out of harmony with the doctrine as well as the genius and polity of our Church, both alike ridiculing a strict enforcement of discipline, determined that Bishop Orwig must be supplanted by Rev. S. Neitz, as bishop of the Evangelical Association.

Between 1848 and 1863, however, great changes had taken place in the Church. The number of annual conferences had increased from three to nine. The borders of the Church now extended into the "far West", and the personnel of the General Conference was very greatly altered. Instead of being composed almost exclusively of Pennsylvania Germans, as had been the case, the General Conference now included delegates from six other States.

This fact in itself was a formidable obstacle in the way of this faction in the accomplishment of their purpose, and moreover being divided among themselves, both candidates, Orwig and Neitz being Pennsylvanians, for the first time in the history of the Church, a bishop failed of a re-election, and Rev. J. J. Esher of the Illinois Conference was elected to the office of bishop. However, that he was a western man was not the only offence to this nativistic element, but that he happened to have been born on the other side of the Atlantic, although he came to this country when but seven years of age, was a still greater offence. For this reason, and because he had been elected in preference to Rev. S. Neitz, who was the leader and especial favorite of the faction in the East, Bishop Esher was much disliked and opposed by them from the beginning of his episcopacy. In 1890, Rev. M. J. Carothers, formerly a member of the Central Pa. Conference, and for many years its acknowledged leader, said in the Publishing House in Cleveland, O., that he had "commenced to rebel 27 years ago." This agrees exactly with the date of Bishop Esher's election. Moreover within the bounds of the East Pa. Conference Bishop Esher's style, manner, and in fact almost everything he said and did, was privately made the subject of adverse criticism, and his influence circumscribed and injured wherever it was possible to do so by Rev. S. Neitz and his intimate personal followers. The writer knows whereof he speaks. Under the influences dominant in that conference in those days, not only were unfavorable remarks made against and about the bishops, their work and their office belittled, but reflections cast upon our missionary arrangements and suspicions aroused against the management of our Publishing House, so that young ministers were led to regard the general officers of the Church as persons who at least needed a great deal of watching.

At a certain camp-meeting, Rev. R. Yeakel, who was then Corresponding Secretary of the Missionary Society, was also present. The remarks made concerning him by the presiding elder were anything but gentlemanly and complimentary, so that the writer became disgusted, and could not help believing that there was some purpose on the elder's part. The presiding elder, S. Neitz, also absolutely refused to arrange appointments for the Corresponding Secretary on his district. Surely the elements of disloyalty were largely present in this conference, years ago.

Whereas erroneous statements have been made in reference to the election of bishops in 1863, a statement taken from the official records may not be out of place: Bishop J. Long was re-elected on the first ballot, receiving fifty-two votes out of a total of sixty-three. On the second ballot there was no election.

It was then resolved that all the candidates be dropped excepting Orwig, Esher and Neitz. There was no election either on the third ballot, after which Orwig withdrew his name. The fourth ballot then resulted in the election of Rev. J. J. Esher, having received thirty-five votes out of a total of sixty-two. One of the sixty-three delegates declined to vote after Orwig had withdrawn his name.

At the General Conference held in Pittsburgh, Pa., in 1867, charges were again preferred against Rev. S. Neitz for erroneous teaching on the doctrine of holiness. The committee to which the charges were preferred, reported that Bro. Neitz had used expressions, phrases and figures of speech, of which they strongly disapproved; but that according to the explanation he had given, it did not seem to them that he had intended to teach doctrine contrary to the faith of our Church. The editor of the General Conference Journal, Rev. C. G. Koch, gave Rev. S. Neitz permission to write out the explanation he had made to the General Conference upon which he had been exonerated. Into this written explanation, which Neitz demanded must be published in the journal precisely as he had written it, he inserted a very ugly personal attack upon Bishop Esher, and also a similar attack upon the doctrine of entire sanctification as taught in our Book of Discipline, *neither of which he had included in his address before the General Conference, and upon which he had been acquitted.* Moreover this was done in the face of the fact that at that very General Conference Neitz had voted for a declaration drawn up by Bishop Esher, fully and unconditionally endorsing the doctrine of holiness as taught in our Discipline. Both of the bishops, as it was their duty to do, protested vigorously against the course pursued by Rev. Neitz. Bishop Long did so publicly in the *Botschafter* and Bishop Esher at the session of the East Pa. Conference at its session, held in Reading, Pa. The conference being in full sympathy with Neitz, treated the protest with contempt. The writer well remembers the sarcastic speeches with which it was greeted.

The result was a bitter, sarcastic attack upon both of the bishops by Rev. S. Neitz, in the *Botschafter* in what is known as "*Sporadisches*". That Rev. R. Dubs, who was then editor of the *Botschafter*, should publish such an outrageous attack upon the bishops, occasioned much surprise and comment at the time, the future history, however, of the man, as will be developed in this volume, affords a full solution of the riddle. Finally at the session of the East Pa. Conference, held in Philadelphia, Pa., in 1869, charges were preferred against Rev. S. Neitz, by Rev. H. Stoetzel, in which the above cited facts were set forth. There was no doubt whatever as to the alleged facts. Of this the committee, to which the charges were referred, was thoroughly convinced.

There was not even a decent excuse for Neitz's personal attack upon Bishop Esher, and much less for his attack upon our doctrines. He himself could not defend his course in inserting in his written speech, which purported to be the speech he had made before the General Conference, what he had not said, and would not have ventured to say by any means, —more especially as the Journal said he had been exonerated from the charge of heresy upon the explanations made in that speech. The committee and the conference, however, feared the influence which he had acquired through his eloquence,— feared a schism, should he be declared guilty and be dealt with as he had deserved,—and so agreed upon a report which was intentionally so worded as not to say anything. Great pains were taken and a good deal of foolscap spoiled until the report had been formulated. The report was adopted, and the schism averted, but the slanders against the bishops, who had stood up for the Church and her doctrines, and the fearful attack upon our Discipline remained, *without being corrected.*

Probably no more offensive and unjust attack was ever made before or since upon our doctrine than had been made by Rev. S. Neitz. He declared that he had often been *ashamed* of the doctrine of sin as taught in our Discipline, and that he would be *ashamed* to teach as Bishop Esher had in an article written for the *Evangelical Messenger*, and fully in accord with the doctrine of sin as taught by our Church. And what was still worse, Neitz had never said these things, and would not have had the moral courage to say them, in his speech before the General Conference, but had falsely incorporated them in his written speech. He had been acquitted of the charge of heresy because of the explanations made in his speech before the General Conference, but in his written and printed speech, which, of course, was to be an exact reproduction of what he had said, he not only falsifies, but makes a much uglier attack upon our doctrine than in the sermon upon which the charge of heresy had been based!

The conference after all seemed to feel that it had not done the fair thing, and so subsequently it passed a resolution of confidence in the integrity and honesty of the bishops, whom the persons the conference had exonerated, had so fiercely assailed! The injury however, was done, and the great wrong was never righted. It has borne and is still to-day bearing its fruit of discord and disharmony.

However Rev. S. Neitz was not the only agitator. Rev. T. G. Clewell, the editor of the *Evangelical Messenger*, who had also voted for the declarations of the General Conference, made in Pittsburg, in 1867, was a faithful ally of his eastern co-worker in undermining the Church. In a series of articles on the doctrine of sanctification he most adroitly assailed not only this doctrine, but our articles of faith in general, so that charges were preferred against him, in consequence of which he resigned as editor. It has already been stated how in his revolutionary course he was sustained by the East Pa. Conference, as also virtually by the Central and the Pittsburg. However, not only were these public attacks made, but privately the work of calumniation was also carried on to a large extent; in the pulpit and out of it insinuations were made against the chief officers of the Church, more especially however against the bishops. Instances, if space would permit, could be given almost without number. One may suffice. Rev. D. Yuengst, a bosom friend of Bishop Dubs, at whose house he stopped during the General Conference of 1883 in Allentown, Pa., preached a sermon on Lehigh Circuit in which he publicly assailed the general officers of the Church. One of the principal members of that circuit says in a letter to the writer: "Rev. D. Yuengst was the first preacher I heard say anything in public against our Publishing House and our bishops. Bro. Neitz sometimes did so privately, but I never heard him say anything publicly." At a camp-meeting held under the supervision of Rev. J. O. Lehr on Pleasant Valley Circuit in 1876 the entire private conversation among the ministers favorable to the ideas entertained by the presiding elder was against the General Conference held the year previous and the bishops etc. Rev. W. H. Baker in a sermon even publicly insinuated against the action of the General Conference, simply because the friends of Rev. S. Neitz had again been defeated in their plans to make him bishop,

These facts—and their number might be increased almost indefinitely—demonstrate that the opposition to the general government of our Church, and especially towards the bishops, dates its origin back a good many years, and that it was the outgrowth of two causes. First the conception that whereas the Church had her origin in Pennsylvania she must continue to be governed by ideas peculiar to Pennsylvania, and especially that Pennsylvanians only should control her destiny. This would have been pardonable to a certain extent under the circumstances, had not men whose personal ambition had been disappointed used this feeling for their personal aggrandizement and against the unity and peace of the Church. Secondly, a disagreement with the doctrine of the Church in reference to entire sanctification. This was the case not only with a majority of the ministers of the East Pa. Conference, but also with very many of those who joined the ranks of the seceders in the

Central Pa., the Pittsburg, the Illinois, the Iowa, the Des Moines and the Platte River Conferences. In fact with but few exceptions the leaders of the secession movement never believed nor preached the doctrine of holiness as taught by our Church. To mention their names is sufficient evidence: M. J. Carothers, J. D. Dorner, E. L. Kiplinger, John Schneider, D. B. Byers, D. H. Kooker, C. W. Anthony, J. Henn etc. Rev. D. B. Byers wrote what he called a review of the action of the General Conference of 1867 on the doctrine in question in which he strongly declared against it, and for the writing of which Bishop Long preferred charges against him. In order to save himself ecclesiastically Byers recalled all he had written, and apologized for his attack upon the General Conference and our doctrines.

In order that the reader may see the spirit which even at that time pervaded "the fathers of the present secession movement", several anonymous letters written to Bishop Joseph Long in those days are herewith given. It will be seen that the spirit of "those fathers" descended upon the sons. That their writings breathe exactly the same spirit, and in fact are identical in language with the writings of those who in these latter days openly rebelled against the Church, as "Heil's Facts", and the "Evangelical" and "Allgemeine" abundantly prove. "By their fruits ye shall know them."

The first of these letters is given exactly as it is written, orthography and punctuation. It is evident that the misspelling was done for a purpose.

"Shame, Shame: for an Old man like you to publish and Slander such a worthy man Like our Bro. Neitz. You certainly ought to resign from your office And prepare for Eternity or you will certainly end in Hell. You have broke your Old neck for ever in our Society. You ought to have know that you were only Elected to Bishopry to honor Your age; for Bishop no conference that I have heard off Either West or East have at anytime spoke well of you they all spoke of seeing to much Esel (mule) about you: And now the world knows it for you have left the beast out of the stable. You perhaps think the West would sustain you, but let me tell you in plain words, no Christian, no honest, and moral man will nor can sustain you, it takes an un-Godly man to favor such treatment or perhaps an Extra Sanctifyed one like W. W. and the Ring at Cleveland, Why you appear like King Saul "An alle die es angeht." (To whom it may concern.) I guess very few care anything about, And very few believe Mr. Orwig's humbugery and none of us preach it: I was told the Cleveland ring said that as soon as Mr. Esher would come back then a charge would be brought against Bro. Neitz. Well I would do so to if I would be in your place, then I would let Mr. Esher bring the charge you act chairman and appoint the Extra and Exbishop Orwig and the Grosardiga Dubs and the Fussegungle Reuben der Grosse or his brother Jesse in the East as Committee then proceed and the Devils in Hell shall rejoice.

But mind Old Fellow we are ready for you. You have deserved the penetentery. You can go ahead but let me tell you before Neitz is put out you and some of the Cleveland ring will be out. We sustain Neitz a good many of us in the West, And his Conf. will any how that I have ascertained. Meanwhile I Will return your Valentine and black ball it, As I dont recognize it any longer as the Photograph of a Bishop but as an old "Sturkopf" (old Obstinate).

The writer by inserting a sentence as if the letter had been written somewhere in the West hoped thereby to mislead the bishop and to shield the East, *where it was written*, from the disgrace of sending such a letter to so venerable a man as Bishop Long. Not only is it known that this shameful epistle was written in the East, but there is also very little doubt as to the person who wrote it. This abuse was heaped upon Bishop Long simply because he believed it to be his duty to defend our doctrine and discipline as one of the chief pastors of the church against the attacks made upon them by Solomon Neitz.

The following letter, also anonymous, was written in the German language. A translation, as nearly literal as it can well be made is submitted.

"Preacher J. Lang. Your blackguard article which appeared in the *Botschafter* (in reference to our worthy Brother S Neitz) was read by me and many others with surprise; for such a shameless unchristian article filled with malice we would not have expected from any other member of the Cleveland Whiskey Ring, but not from you as Bishop. But through this fearful act, so similar to Pius (Pope) of Rome that if one would not know anything of Bishop Long, one would be compelled to believe the production was one of the miserable Papal Bulls issued from Rome. You together with your Brother Esher have not dealt with Neitz in accordance with God's order. Thus I hear at least from all who are acquainted with your treachery and deception and plans, yes preachers and laymen say so. I have even heard of one preacher who spoke of your.................. He said you ought to have died first, you as an old man with one foot in the grave, near the end of your course, thus to appear in public, and so fearfully to condemn a man who is worthy of all honor and respect, and from his youth up was only a blessing to the Evangelical Association, and is still so up to the present day.

This man (Neitz) can be used everywhere. He is a man of honor in every respect. He preaches God's word purely. He preaches Christian perfection and sanctification according to God's word, and clear, and the best of it is that he lives it also.* He can be compared with any of your crazy holiness fanatics in Cleveland or anywhere else. For their holiness preaching is unscriptural, and besides they do not live it, one must be ashamed of them.

Brother Lang. W. W. Orwig, the poor man, whom we know for many years. It would be good for him were he to lay down his office and use the rest of his time to prepare for eternity. This man wanted to kill off Neitz this long time, but could not do it, hence he now uses Bishop Lang as his tool to throttle Neitz. Orwig lies in the pit, Lang wants to dig still deeper, because he is a bigger man, one sees nothing of him now any more but his head. He ,has sunk deep enough already. But what is going to happen, the dear old man wants to make things still worse. For God's sake dont bury yourself before you die. Save your honor and cease your cursing. I want to tell you yet that if you will not recall your blackguard article you need not again come to the East to preach for us. We do not want to hear you. Dont think that I am writing for myself only, such feelings you will find throughout the East among our members. You cannot kill off Neitz. He is the man for the people. The people hang at him like a burr at ones clothes. He has become more friends through your cursing than he had before.

(LAYMAN.)

Do not these letters clearly show that what has been stated about this faction in the East being out of harmony with our doctrine of sanctification is true? It was even made a subject of ridicule and those preaching and confessing it were persecuted, whilst the man, Rev. S. Neitz, who declared over his own signature that he had often been ashamed of our doctrine is lauded to the skies and presented as a man whom the people will follow. Nor can the intelligent reader fail to notice that because Bishop Long defended our discipline he is called a "pope" and he and others accused of the purpose of "killing" and "throttling" Neitz, and all this because they did not allow Neitz to go on unmolested in his work of undermining our doctrine and discipline and in defying the authority of the church. How very much like the language of R. Dubs in his *Allgemeine* and of various writers in the *Evangelical*. The same spirit of lawlessness, of persecution, of disrespect for authority and government pervades the disloyal faction of to-day, and finds expression in the same language.

Probably it should be added that the above letter was not written by a layman, but by a minister, and that there is very little doubt, judging from the handwriting, as to who the author is.

As still further evidence of the correctness of that statement that S. Neitz and his following were out of harmony with the doctrines of our church a few extracts from a letter written by said Neitz to our Bishop Seybert are herewith given. It seems that he labored under the impression that he might possibly even convert the bishop to his views. Knowing very well if that could be accomplished it would be a long step in the direction of erasing the chapter an the doctrine of sanctification from our discipline.

Neitz wrote as follows.

"The English or Wesleyan theology is shallow and superficial. Superficiality is characteristic of the English people, which can be seen in the fact that they allow themselves to be governed by a woman. German theology, however, is solid and thorough, German theologians are thinkers, they take an exalted position, and take a high flight; German theology in a few years will take precedence over the English, and will drive it from the field. After Wesley was converted he realized the necessity of becoming better instructed in theology, hence he traveled to

Germany to Count Zinzendorf, of whom he learned a great deal, and upon his return, he acted in a measure like the hedge-sparrow in the fable, which hid himself in the feathers of an eagle, who in his flight had soared above all others, when the rogue sallied from his hiding place, and flew still a little higher, and then sang his zitterritter attadat. Upon his return from Zinzendorf, Wesley set up his extra sanctification doctrine, but the doctrine will not last very long."

Is any more evidence needed to prove that Neitz and his faction were disloyal to the doctrines of our church? However not only were he and his followers disloyal to its doctrine, but to its polity as well. They were very much more in favor of a congregational system of church government than of the associated or episcopal form because they themselves could not control it. The episcopal office was antagonized and even ridiculed, and its duties and responsibilities and authority belittled at every possible opportunity. Hence in the beginning of the present phase of our difficulties in the East these old, deep-seated prejudices against the episcopal office were aroused with all the energy of which the leaders were capable, raising the cry "we need no bishops." During our present sad litigation every effort possible is made to circumscribe the authority and power of the bishops and magnify the powers and authority of the presiding elders—even arguing that the office of presiding elder in our church is superior in dignity and power to that of the bishop! They even argued that our entire itinerant system is at variance with the laws of Pennsylvania, and that all denominations having this system must reconstruct their church government in order to conform with the laws of the State! Folly.

These things would have been impossible for the flippant young men who have manipulated things in the East, in order, as Master Wood, who heard the cases in Allentown, says, "to organize the annual conference of 1891 upon a pre-concerted plan in which they totally repudiated and ignored the regularly constituted authorities of the church,"— had not Solomon Neitz lived before them, and thoroughly cultivated the ground and sown the seed of dissension, opposition, and disloyalty. The writer regrets that the truth of history demands that these things must be stated, as Rev. S. Neitz was not only a fine orator, but in many other respects an estimable man ; but facts are facts nevertheless.

However, the tares could never have grown to such an extent had not later a bishop of the Evangelical Association appeared on the scene, nursing the fires into new life, and afterwards, for personal purpose united this eastern element with the western malcontents into one sinew of rebellion against the law, order and authority of the church.

As the memory of our sainted Bishop Long has been insulted by some of the disloyal element by the insinuation that if he were living he would be with them in their anarchistic proceedings the following letter is inserted :

"At home, Oct. 14, 1868.

Dear Friend in the Lord, J. J. Esher :

Grace and peace from God to you and yours. By the help of God I came home safe, but am very tired, and must rest for a few days. Since we parted I have been thinking that probably you had misunderstood me in reference to the next sessions of the annual conferences. I am not of the opinion that the plan need be published, I only wanted an understanding between us how we want to hold them. The Michigan ought to be appointed, and the Kansas ought to be appointed a week earlier. (Hence it seems Bishop Long also believed the bishops might appoint and change the time for holding annual conferences.—*Editor*.) Let it be understood beforehand that I will not attend the East Pa. Conference unless I shall be legally cited to be there, and in case Neitz's affairs will come up, count upon it beforehand that they will declare you just as guilty as Neitz. (This, however, I shall very much regret, for I hold you to be entirely innocent in the affair.) I do not write what I presume, but I write what I know, and so you will no doubt be compelled to enter into a compromise with them, and then Neitz will again come out clean, and continue to carry on his disturbance unhindered. And then in addition they will investigate the General Conference officers, the bishops not excepted, find them guilty and condemn them! What has been done in the Neitz affair? I presume nothing has been done, and the whole affair will be left to the East Pa. Conference, which assumes to be a kind of General Conference and can act for the entire Association. Perhaps, however, I am too hasty in my judgment. I will in the meanwhile leave the matter with the Lord and hope for the best. Write me soon again.

Yours with great respect and love,
JOSEPH LONG."

Just what the clear-headed and far seeing bishop predicted would happen at the session of the East Pa. Conference did happen. The conference arrogated unto itself the right to sit in judgment upon men who where in no wise responsible to the conference and presumed to act for the entire church. Exactly as the conference again did in 1871, and as it did in Pottsville in 1889, and in Shamokin in 1890, and as a faction of that conference did in Allentown, Pa., in 1891, — namely arrogate unto itself to sit in judgment even upon the legality of the action of the General Conference of 1887, nullifying said action and issuing a call for a " General Conference " of their own. Nullification came first, then secession. Just as if some justice of the peace in Weissenberg Township, in the county of Lehigh, Pa., were to attempt to pass upon the legality of the acts of the court of Common Pleas in and for the county of Lehigh ; or the court of Common Pleas of Lehigh county were to pass upon the legality and constitutionality of the acts and decisions of the Supreme Court of Pennsylvania !

However it is but just to say that during all these conflicts in the East Pa. Conference there was a strong minority both of preachers and people who where firm and outspoken in their adherence both to the doctrines and polity of our church, and who have stood with unflinching loyalty by all her interests throughout the entire conflict to this time, and that too in the face of much opposition and even persecution.

CHAPTER II.

Rudolph Dubs is elected Bishop in order "to put Esher down," and the results following.

We found the first root of our difficulties in Pennsylvania. The second we shall find in Illinois. As has been heretofore stated both Rev. John Schneider and Rev. D. B. Byers, two of the leading ministers in the Illinois Conference in later years, were not in harmony with our doctrine of holiness. They were also at no time in favor of a strict enforcement of discipline, claiming to be "liberal" in all things. For these and other reasons they were unfriendly to Bishop Esher, who always stood firmly and squarely by our discipline and its enforcement. They were however very intimate friends of Rev. R. Dubs, who was then editor of the *Botschafter*. It was well known that Bishop Esher's strength and influence was so great in the church that his re-election could not be avoided. However, it was whispered around in Philadelphia at the General Conference in 1875, "while we cannot defeat him, let us cut his vote down as much as possible." While the opponents of Bishop Esher knew they were numerically too weak to defeat his re-election they at least comforted themselves in having found a man in the person of R. Dubs, of whom they seemed to feel confident, that in due time he would be able to destroy and supplant the influence of the senior bishop. After Rev. R. Dubs was elected one of the bishops in 1875, the enemies of Bishop Esher, East and West, rejoiced greatly that at last "he (Esher) had found his match," and that now, he "would be put down." Such statements were freely made at the time, Bishop Dubs himself acknowledged this to be true in the writer's house in Allentown, Pa., during the session of the General Conference in 1883, he then said: "*The greatest mistake of my life is that at the time of my election to the episcopal office, I resolved to put Bishop Esher down, and that I continued to act in this manner.*" Bishop Dubs made the same confession to Rev. R. Yeakel, although he was either childish or wicked enough to put the blame for the course he had pursued upon another, in which attempt he made himself guilty of a positive falsehood. Bishop Dubs made the same confession, only as it appears, omitting the "greatest," in a conversation in Minnesota between himself and several other brethren, which can be substantiated whenever it may become necessary.

That those who voted to make R. Dubs one of the bishops, with the purpose in view, of "putting Esher down," were not mistaken in their man, became painfully evident already, at that very General Conference session. Complaint had been brought to the General Conference, that the subscription lists of the Publishing House had been used by some one for improper purposes. The matter was referred to the committee on the Publishing House, which in due time reported that these lists were sacred and were not to be used for any other purpose than for that for which they were sent in, and instructed the Publishing Agent to bring the offender to trial. While the report was under discussion Bishop Dubs made a strong speech in its favor denouncing the person guilty of such conduct in vigorous language, and yet it was afterwards discovered *that Bishop Dubs himself was the guilty party.* Had the instructions of the General Conference of 1875 been carried out Dubs would already then have been placed under charges and convicted not only of what the General Conference considered a gross offence, but of deception as well. The reader will find in this episode a key with which to unlock the future. The church had been unfortunate in electing an unprincipled man to the highest office in her gift. Immediately after Dub's election, Rev. W. F. Schneider, a man of sound judgment, of unimpeachable character, esteemed and honored throughout the entire Church, made the following remark: "*We now have a man for bishop in our Church with a conscience like indiarubber, elastic enough to stretch or to shrink as may best suit his own purposes, and I apprehend it will not be at all long before* WOE *will come upon the Evangelical Association.*"

Probably no other man knew R. Dubs better than Rev. W. F. Schneider, as they had been associated together in the Publishing House. His words sound like a prophecy. The "woe" came very shortly indeed. Dubs had scarcely entered into his new office before the trouble commenced. How could it be otherwise, when as he himself had confessed, his purpose was to put down his senior in office?

It will be necessary to show in this work how energetically Bishop Dubs devoted himself to the task which he had undertaken. Of course it will be impossible to state everything in this connection. The recital must be confined to the more important acts connected with the sad career of this unfortunate man. Moreover it will appear that these things mostly happened during the first eight years of Dubs' episcopal career. At the end of that time he seems to have been thoroughly convinced that he undertook too large a contract, and thence forward his entire aim seemed to be how to save himself from the consequences of the suicidal course he had pursued. He had sown to the wind and the returning whirlwind threatened to overwhelm him with sorrow and disgrace.

Not very long after his election a brother was selected by the Executive Committee of the Board of Missions as missionary to Germany. In such cases the committee usually attaches great weight to the opinion of the bishops, as these very frequently are the only persons in the committee personally acquainted with the proposed candidates. The merits and demerits of the persons under consideration are of course stated and discussed, it having always been understood that such discussions are wholly confidential, just as are the discussions connected with the stationing of the ministers. In the case above alluded to, Bishop Esher who knew the brother in question very well, — in fact was intimately acquainted with him, and a firm personal friend, frankly stated the brother's qualifications, but also alluded to one or two things which might be to his disadvantage, yet heartily recommending his appointment, and concurring in it.

Later on when this brother took leave of his conference, Bishop Esher offered a resolution expressing the love and esteem in which the brother was held, and also made a few parting remarks. Soon afterwards Bishop Dubs traveled through Illinois, and hearing what Bishop Esher had said and the resolution he had offered, he said: "In the session of the Executive Committee Esher said brother H. was unfit and unsuited for Germany, and here he offered such resolutions." The purpose of such remarks is very evident. It was to lower Bishop Esher in the opinion of the brethren, and to reflect upon his sincerity. There could be no other purpose. However in addition it was a gross violation of official confidence, and what was even much worse, Bishop Dubs' statement was untrue.

The next item in this connection will be somewhat lengthy, so that the reader's indulgence is craved; truth demands that the circumstances be stated somewhat in detail.

Bishop Esher had been requested by the trustees of the Union Biblical Institute, located at Naperville, Ill., to accept the Principalship of that institution, the trustees even declaring that the institution would not be opened unless he would consent to accept the position. He finally consented to accept it upon the condition, that he should not be required to neglect any of his duties as bishop. With this understanding he was elected, and empowered by the trustees to appoint the necessary teachers, as well as to formally open the institute. Upon the request of the Principal the Executive Committee of the Board of Trustees was authorized to assist him in the formal opening of the same. After the Principal became more familiar with the condition of the finances and the affairs of the college he arrived at the conclusion that it would be premature and unwise to open the Institute, and that the better plan would be for the students to pursue theological studies in connection with the College as had been done for some years previous. The bishop was also convinced that the Institute needed a man not only thoroughly competent as a teacher, but also one of ripe experience in the itinerant labor of our Church, and such a one did not seem to be available at that time. Notwithstanding these things, the Principal had arranged with the Executive Committee to open the Institute upon a certain fixed time. An accident on the railroad prevented him from being present.

Word was sent to the Executive Committee by the Bishop informing them of the reason for his absence and offering to come the following day. The committee, notwithstanding the Principal's enforced absence, without any authority whatever, and without informing the Principal, went through a certain ceremony which they called an opening, and then published in the *Messenger* that the Institute had been opened. The Principal knowing nothing whatever of the so-called opening of the Institute and believing that the editor had been misinformed, sent him a note correcting what he considered an error. Hereupon the Bishop was not only fiercely assailed in the *Messenger*, but also a spirit of opposition to him was assiduously cultivated among the students. The reader will bear in mind that John Schneider and William Huelster were members of this Executive Committee, and in fact constituted the same. Later on it will be shown how they and R. Dubs were in league to put Esher down, and that this Institute affair was a part of the program. In a letter written to Bishop Esher by John Schneider, about this time, he declared that he would not appear in the *Messenger* against the Bishop, as he did not propose to take chestnuts out of the fire for others, from which it appears some one else was connected with this scheme, and yet very soon afterwards a terrific onslaught upon the Bishop appeared in the *Messenger*, signed by the Executive Committee. These onslaughts upon the bishop were continued in that paper long after he ceased to reply. At this time Rev. J. Hartzler was editor of the *Messenger*, and R. Dubs President of the Board of Publication and of its Executive Committee, having practically full control of our publishing interests. They were not slow to use their advantage in the interest of their faction, and their one great purpose, namely "to put Esher down".

After teachers for the institute had been appointed facts came to the knowledge of Bishop Esher which made it impossible for him to remain connected with it, should the services of one of the appointed teachers be continued. His purpose was quietly to withdraw without creating any disturbance. He considered it right, however, that the Executive Committee should know his reasons for withdrawing, hence he communicated the knowledge in his possession, *confidentially* to two members of the committee. They, however, violated the confidence reposed in them by the Bishop, and thereby greatly intensified the feeling already existing. This same teacher, concerning whose moral conduct, Bishop Esher had informed those two members of the Executive Committee, but which was of such a character and the circumstances that the Bishop's hands were tied, was nevertheless kept in his place by the Committee. Subsequently after a regular trial he was dismissed from his position in Naperville, Ill., for unchristian conduct, the charges, however, did not include the crime of which the Executive Committee had been informed.

During these difficulties, the same parties above mentioned, namely John Schneider and Wm. Huelster, circulated the report that Bishop Esher's objections to the appointed teacher arose from his desire to have his son-in-law appointed to the position, although both of them knew that the objections of the bishop were on account of alleged immorality. As evidence for the allegation John Schneider read a letter at a session of the trustees of the Institute in which *as he read it*, this allegation seemed to have been established. J. Schneider not only read the letter in question at this official meeting in this way, but he also read it to the Illinois Conference *in the same way.* This charge so repeatedly made against Bishop Esher, and said to have been substantiated by a letter over his own signature, caused so much confusion that a special session of the trustees of the Institute was called to investigate these accusations. As Bishop Esher's collegues, R. Yeakel and the writer were deeply interested in these accusations made against their senior, they also attended the extra session, in order to become personally acquainted with the facts. Bishop Dubs was in Germany at the time. At this session John Schneider again read the letter above alluded to in the same way he had done before, namely that Bishop Esher desired the appointment of his son-in-law as teacher in the Institute. The Bishop strenuously denied that he had thus written, and declared the letter was read falsely by Schneider. The trustees then demanded that the letter in question be handed to the secretary to be read by him, and also that each member of the Board be given the privilege of a personal examination of the same. The two bishops present asked that they be permitted also to examine the letter which request was granted. To the surprise of every one present it was discovered *that John Schneider had deliberately, for a purpose of his own, as one of the conspirators "to put Bishop Esher down," read the letter falsely, and had thus given false testimony against his neighbor, upon several occasions, and before official bodies.* This false reading was not done because the handwriting was in any way illegible, or that the statements made were not fully and plainly stated, so that a misconstruction could be placed upon the language or an error made on account of the handwriting. The false reading was done deliberately and had so been agreed upon by his co-conspirator William Huelster, who not only consented to this false testimony but publicly and privately declared the same was true. These two men, who thus conspired together to give false testimony against Bishop Esher, and who carried out their wickedness, were the principal witnesses in the sham trials held in Chicago and Reading later on for the purpose of destroying the reputation and influence of the bishops of the Evangelical Association! What are men possessing such a spirit, and such a conscience, and such a character not capable of doing? And these men were and still are the bosom friends of Rudolph Dubs, and his associates in the conspiracy against Bishop Esher, and who, failing to accomplish his downfall, conspired together to destroy the church itself.

It is almost needless to add that the Board of Trustees unanimously adopted resolutions wholly exonerating Bishop Esher from the false and unjust charges which his enemies had circulated against him, and fully sustaining him in the course he had pursued towards the Institute.

In order fully to satisfy the reader of the fact that the letter in question was read falsely by John Schneider several extracts from the proceedings of a so-called "Peace meeting," held in Chicago in 1878, will be added.

"That no evidence has been submitted to prove that Bishop Esher sought or desired the appointment of his son in-law." "That the figure in the letter so often named is *plainly* to be read as figure (1), as it ought to have been read." This report is signed among others by R. Dubs, E. L. Kiplinger, D. B. Byers, D. Kramer, and C. Lindeman, all prominent in the opposition movement, and all testifying by their signatures that John Schneider and William Huelster had not only grossly slandered Bishop Esher, but that they also bore false testimony against him.

The Illinois Conference held its session in the Spring of 1877 in Washington, Ill. This was a year and a half after R. Dubs had been elected bishop. The rumors above mentioned had been circulated throughout the entire conference, as well as to a considerable extent throughout the entire church. Bishop Esher, not being able to be personally present at the conference session, wrote a letter to the conference in reference first to the rumor about the appointment of his son-in-law as a teacher in the Institute, emphatically denying its truthfulness. In a postscript he also reiterated his conviction with reference to the opening of the Institute, assigning as a reason the condition of finances, and gave expression to the idea that probably theological studies might be pursued with equal advantage in the college, the church hardly being able to support two separate and distinct high schools.

This letter was not sent to the chairman, R. Dubs, as Bishop Esher, we shall presently see, had sufficient reason for the belief that that individual had conspired together with John Schneider and William Huelster, two prominent ministers of the Illinois conference to ruin him, hence could not entrust him with the matter. So he placed the letter for the conference in the hands of a trusted friend, with instructions to consult with other brethren in whose friendship and judgment the Bishop placed great confidence. They were to exercise their judgment in reference to the propriety of handing the letter to the conference, the Bishop not being fully decided in his own mind which under the circumstances might be the better course to pursue, bear the slanders silently, or bring the matter to the attention of the conference. These brethren concluded that in justice to the Bishop and the Institute, and all concerned, the letter should be read to the conference. No sooner was the letter read than it was made the occasion for a terrific onslaught upon the bishop, *in his absence*, not only by members of the conference, but also by his colleague in office, the comparatively youthful chairman, R. Dubs. He was serving his first term in the episcopal office, yet in the presence of ministers and people, in the absence of his colleague and senior in office, whom as far as truth would permit he should have defended, and whom as chairman he should have allowed no one else to attack, he publicly fiercely assailed with all the energy at his command. In a speech probably lasting twenty minutes, thoroughly prepared, being delivered from manuscript, he charged his senior colleague with duplicity, with improper motives, and with endangering the existence of an Institution of the church by the course he was pursuing, appealing to the conference to stand up for the Institute and to save it from being crushed by its principal, the senior bishop of the church! Is it a wonder that there is trouble in our beloved church when one of its bishops just elected deliberately pursues such a course towards his colleague and senior in office?

It might be well to inquire what great wrong Bishop Esher had done that made such a course necessary on the part of Bishop Dubs. He had written a letter to his conference of which he had been a member for many years, and in which he had been grossly slandered, protesting his innocence. Afterwards, as already shown above, R. Dubs himself acknowledged Bishop Esher's innocency of those accusations. Furthermore he in a postscript to his letter simply made suggestions in reference to an Institution of which he was Principal and in which he certainly had as much interest as any one else. For making these suggestions he was assailed not only by members of the conference, by permission of the chair, but also by the chairman himself! How does such a course accord with the liberty demanded by R. Dubs and his associates? Simply for suggesting what did not harmonize with his own views he *publicly* and *officially*, from the chair of the conference, assails the motives and honesty of his senior in office! This is the person who afterwards, when the war which he commenced threatened to overwhelm him with defeat and disgrace, posed as the apostle of peace, and as the defender of liberty against tyranny and despotism!

Concerning this remarkable deliverance, William Huelster wrote to one of our ministers, under date of April 23, 1877, very soon after the session: "You ought to have been at our conference session, when Bishop Dubs delivered his written speech against the letter and position of J. J. Esher on the Institute question. It was a masterpiece! Not one of the friends of the principal, J. J. Esher, answered a word, and I corroborated Dubs' speech in the interests of the Institute. This has naturally come to the ears of the Principal and hence he desires a meeting of the Board on his account to explain himself. I do not believe that we owe it to him in view of his unseemly behavior in this matter. He has now found his match (who can master him) in Bishop Dubs." Signed Wm. Huelster.

Of course Wm. Huelster "corroborated Dubs' speech". This was an opportunity for the conspirators such as they would not have soon again for destroying Bishop Esher's influence in the "great Illinois Conference". The best possible use is made of the opportunity. "Not one of the friends of the Principal, J. J. Esher answered a word," says Huelster. How could they? They were dumb-founded, overwhelmed. The other one in the conspiracy, John Schneider, is at hand with Bishop Esher's own letter which he reads not only to prove that his assertions regarding the bishop wanting to have his son-in-law appointed in the Institute were true, but also proving the Bishop guilty of falsehood in writing to the conference denying that he had done so. No wonder they succeeded in breaking down Bishop Esher's influence in his home conference! The wickedness of these three men, R. Dubs, John Schneider and Wm. Huelster in this conspiracy "to put down Esher" has probably no parallel in Church history, remembering the fact that all three were professed ministers of the Gospel, and one of them a bishop in our Church. Bishop Dubs had seen the letter which John Schneider was reading in the conference of which he was chairman as evidence against his colleague; he knew John Schneider was reading it falsely; he knew then as well as he knew it at the subsequent "peace-meeting" in Chicago; he also knew it was doing its work of destruction. By his silence he became a partner in this wicked piece of work. I would again call the attention of the reader to the fact that this trio, R. Dubs, John Schneider and Wm. Huelster, were the principal witnesses in the so-called trials held against the bishops of the Evangelical Association in the cities of Chicago and Reading.

Previous to the session of the Illinois Conference in 1877, John Schneider and Wm. Huelster were in favor of having an extra session of the Board of Trustees of the Institute; but after that remarkable session, where in the absence of Bishop Esher, their purpose had been accomplished by the efficient aid of R. Dubs, they wanted no extra session, as the above letter of Wm. Huelster abundantly proves. They knew very well that at the Board they would be brought face to face with the wronged bishop, and that the facts would be brought out, whereas they wanted things to remain as they had "fixed" them at the conference session, and the injury which had been done to Bishop Esher to go on unchecked. Bishop Dubs was of the same mind with his friends. Previous to starting for Germany, about this time, he wrote to Bishop Bowman warning him to be careful what position he would assume, and if an extra session of the Institute Board was called not to attend it, adding "the great Illinois Conference has spoken." This was true. Under the influence of his remarkable speech, assailing his colleague, the Illinois Conference passed resolutions censuring Bishop Esher for expressing his views concerning the opening of the Institute! Bishop Esher was Principal of the Institute, was a member of the Illinois Annual Conference, but cannot be present on account of official duties elsewhere, presuming that the affairs of the Institute will come up before the body for discussion, suggests in a postscript to a letter that probably it might be prudent in view of the financial condition of the College and Institute to postpone the formal opening of the latter; Bishop Rudolph Dubs, the man who claims to have been the great apostle of liberty in the Evangelical Association influences the conference of which he is chairman to pass a resolution of censure against his absent colleague for expressing an opinion!

At the following session of the General Conference held in 1879, in Chicago, Ill., the proceedings of the Illinois Conference came up for approval and in reference to the action censuring Bishop Esher the following resolution was adopted by that body:

"Whereas, the Principal of the U. B. Institute wrote a letter to the annual session of the Illinois Conference, giving therein under the heading 'Postscript' his advice and views in regard to the U. B. Institute, whereupon said conference passed certain resolutions which according to our opinion place the Principal and his position to the Institute in an unfavorable light, and, Inasmuch as these resolutions contain a censure against a brother not amenable at the bar of said conference, and were passed in his absence, therefore, Resolved, that they be herewith declared illegal and shall be erased."

This action of the General Conference has been quoted to show that the foregoing representations are in full accord with the facts, and further also to show how from the beginning of the difficulties in Illinois, in Pennsylvania, and elsewhere, individual rights, as well as the law of the Church were totally disregarded, if thereby in the opinion of the chief actors in this drama their purposes could be accomplished.

For the first time, probably, in the history of the Church was the theory of so-called annual conference rights, namely that the annual conferences were sovereign and hence had the right to say and do whatsoever they saw fit, publicly argued and defended on the floor of the General Conference, while the action annulling the proceedings of the Illinois Conference concerning Bishop Esher was pending. But an overwhelming majority held that in accordance with our discipline the General Conference is the Supreme Court of law in the Church, and that it shall decide upon the legality of all acts of annual conferences, and hence ordered the illegal and unjust action of the Illinois conference to be erased from its record.

For the first time also in the history of the Church was it apparent that an organized "minority" existed, whose purpose it was to gain control of the Church by any means possible. This "minority" then as afterwards had its strength in the Illinois, East Pa., Central Pa., Pittsburg and Des Moines Conferences. The Platte River and the Oregon were then parts of the Des Moines and Pacific Conferences respectively. Within the bounds of these conferences its work of ruin and devastation has mostly been done. Outside of these named its destroying influence has succeeded only to a very limited extent.

As Bishop Dubs had been the chief instigator of the illegal and unjust resolutions passed by the Illinois Conference in 1877, heretofore alluded to, and had declared to Bro. George Vetter privately at said session that an annual conference could pass any resolutions it pleased ; as he had been so courageous in his attacks upon Bishop Esher in the latter's absence, and had declared privately at that session, that he would have said exactly what he did, "had Esher been present" ; it was expected he would at the General Conference, defend his course and especially the action of the conference, over which he presided, with all the ability and energy at his command. But, instead of defending his course, or pointing out the great wrong of which Bishop Esher had been guilty, and how it became his duty to appeal to the conference to take a firm stand in behalf of an institution of the Church the senior bishop was "crushing," he sat with his face toward the wall, without venturing to speak a word, during the entire discussion, too cowardly to defend his course and too dishonest manfully to acknowledge his great wrong in a Christian spirit. Had Bishop Esher been guilty of attempting to force a member of his own family into a position against the will of the Executive Committee, and failing in this, had then sought to crush the institution he had desired to use for his personal benefit, it would certainly have afforded Bishop Dubs rare opportunity for the display of his oratorical abilities ; and his entire course proves that he would not have been slow in using the occasion. But in Chicago, at the General Conference, Bishop Esher was present to defend himself. That made all the difference in the world. Moreover Bishop Dubs knew that he and his co-conspirators, John Schneider and Wm. Huelster had used false testimony at Washington, Ill., which could not and dare not be used again. *Rudolph Dubs knew silence was his only salvation.* This policy he has chosen to pursue whenever the facts are against him, whenever he knows he cannot defend himself. Whenever he can he has always defended himself. He is the "meek, silent sufferer" only when he knows that the facts and the evidence are against him, and only then.

Although the General Conference declared the action of the Illinois Annnual Conference illegal and ordered it to be erased, thus vindicating Bishop Esher, as he had already been vindicated by the trustees of the Institute; still the great injury which had been done by R. Dubs and his associates only eternity will reveal. From this time onward until the division came in 1890 the Illinois Conference was simply an ecclesiastical political machine in which the offices were parcelled out by a ring to those who would most faithfully carry out its purposes and do its bidding. The upbuilding of the church and the salvation of souls were evidently secondary matters. Ill-will, prejudice and dissatisfaction were engendered against Bishop Esher in particular, and against all others in general who would not allow themselves to be used for the accomplishment of their one great aim and purpose "to put Esher down." By far the larger number of the members in Illinois had completely lost confidence in the integrity of the majority of their ministers. The up-rising of the people in their lay convention, held in Chicago in 1890, abundantly proves this fact, and was a surprise and bitter disappointment to the disloyal ministers of the conference, and most effectually foiled them in their schemes.

So also the course pursued by Bishop Dubs had cost him the confidence of the better portion of the Church, more especially of the leading ministers of the Church. In addition to the sad fact that his integrity and veracity was questioned, especially by those who were near him, so that any statement he made was generally largely discounted if believed at all, the many rumors affecting his chastity had awakened strong suspicions concerning the purity of his character. At this very General Conference Bishop Dubs was compelled to explain his conduct towards a woman on the railroad train between Baltimore, Md., and Washington, D. C. This woman upon leaving the train had charged him to her husband, who was in another car, with insulting conduct, so that he was compelled to flee from the presence of the enraged husband. In his own statements to the General Conference he acknowledged having offered to get her a drink of water, and had touched her person to remind her of something out of place about her dress. The affair was published at the time in several newspapers, among others in the *Pittsburg Despatch*. The fact that Dubs in his explanation and defence, in order to shield himself, found it necessary to say that the woman in question was a disreputable person, which was untrue, only awakened still more distrust in the minds of many. The question was asked by many why did not Bishop Dubs explain the half dozen or more other rumors just as seriously effecting his purity as this incident? The only difference was that these had not been given newspaper publicity. Why also was asked, do these rumors only follow Bishop Dubs and neither of our other bishops who have traveled just as extensively over the same ground?

Having referred to the conspiracy between R. Dubs and John Schneider it may not be amiss to furnish some more facts in evidence concerning the same. On or about the 8th of Nov. 1876, just about a year after Dubs' election as bishop, John Schneider wrote Dubs a letter in which he poured out his soul to his friend Dubs in reference to Bishop Esher. This letter Dubs lost in Wisconsin. Some one found it who believed it to be his duty to inform Bishop Esher of what was being said and done behind his back, and what according to the contents of this letter he might expect from one of his colleagues. The finder of the letter in writing to Bishop Esher uses the following

"That Dubs and Schneider do not appear in that letter as ministers of the Gospel, but as quite different persons is indeed very plain. This they have since still more shown by their conduct. For these reasons I preserved Dubs' postal and noted down the principal points in Schneider's letter. I also had a conversation with Dubs at our conference session concerning the letter, but he upbraided me that I had betrayed him, and had repaid his confidence in me in a dishonorable manner, because I had allowed a brother to read the letter I had found."

The letter contained the following points:

"(1) That Dubs will be met at the depot in Chicago upon his arrival there by Rev. M. Heyl, and that Dubs should try to find out through Heyl what he knew about Bishop Esher's affairs, warning Dubs however to be very careful in his conversation, as Heyl is an intimate friend of Bishop Esher.

(2) Schneider writes "that he hopes Bishop Esher will not find out that he does not want him at the dedication of the new church in Chicago of which Esher and family are members. I know he would like to dedicate it, but I don't want him, but you (Dubs) shall dedicate it. However, I hardly know how to take hold of the matter so that he does not discover that I don't want him."

(3) Schneider says: "I have often brought Esher under the bench and I will get him there again."

The finder of the letter adds, "I would simply add that the letter proves beyond a doubt that Dubs and Schneider occupy a jesuitical attitude towards Bishop Esher."

Another minister familiar with the contents of the letter writes:

"The letter so overwhelmed me with sorrow and indignation that I was unable to sleep for several nights. A man who can write such a letter as John Schneider wrote to Bishop Dubs, must have his heart full of bitter gall, yea full of Satan. And what shall be thought of a bishop who carries about such letters as sweet morsels? The entire tenor of the letter goes to show that Dubs' letters to Schneider must have been of a similar character. The Lord be merciful to our church."

The reader will bear in mind that these things took place only a year after Dubs' election as bishop. Schneider was P. E. of Chicago district and as such was a frequent visitor at the house of Bishop Esher, as such was one of the pastors of his family, and by all appearances very friendly towards Bishop Esher. Not only had he invited Bishop Esher to officiate at the dedication of the church mentioned in the lost letter, but when the Bishop declined, earnestly urged him to do so. "The tenor of the letter," says one who knew its contents, "goes to show that Dubs' letters to Schneider must have been of a similar character." This was but a sample of their correspondence. If Schneider had not known Dubs' feelings and opinion of Bishop Esher he would never have ventured to write as he did. This must be clear to every one. Does not this correspondence and the subsequent acts of Schneider and Dubs in mutually presenting false testimony against Bishop Esher in Washington, Ill., fully prove the conspiracy into which they had entered "to put Esher down?"

In order that the extent may be fully shown to which R. Dubs and J. Schneider have gone to bring their wicked devices to pass, several other items in connection with this last letter must be stated. During a meeting of the trustees of the Institute held in Naperville, Ill., in July 1877, Bishop Esher confronted Schneider with the contents of the letter he had written to Dubs. At first Schneider strenuously denied that the letter contained anything of the kind, finally, however, he admitted the correctness of Bishop Esher's accusations, upon finding that the evidence was in the Bishop's possession, confessing that Dubs had burnt the notorious letter after it again came into his hands. Why burn it if it contained nothing improper? Why not save it and produce it as evidence that the allegations made concerning it were incorrect? The foregoing acknowledgements of John Schneider were made in the presence of Revs. M. Pfitzinger, Joseph Umbach and J. M. Haug.

After the so-called "peace-meeting" held in Chicago on Nov. 15th, 1878, R. Dubs and John Schneider intercepted Bishop Esher as he was leaving the church in which the meeting was held, and insisted upon having an opportunity to explain what was meant in the "lost letter" by the statement that Dubs should try to find out from Rev. M. Heyl something in connection with the Bishop's family. The Bishop, though reluctant to hear their explanation consented finally to listen to their statement. Dubs made the explanation, by saying it referred to a certain letter written by Rev. A. Halmhuber, then a missionary in Japan, which letter Bishop Esher had read to Dubs and Heyl while they were on a visit at the Bishop's house on a previous occasion. That Bishop Esher having stopped very abruptly in his reading they (Dubs and Heyl) were of the opinion that Halmhuber had asked for his daughter in marriage, and that they (Dubs and Schneider) were anxious to find out whether their surmisings were correct or not. This was indeed exalted business for a bishop and a presiding elder! And yet quite in keeping with their character. It is but just to Bro. Halmhuber to add that there was no truth whatever in the suspicions of these two worthies.

John Schneider had already told the untruth in Naperville when he attempted to explain away his letter, now he and R. Dubs conspire and agree to go together to Bishop Esher and attempt to deceive him. Such is usually the course of wicked men, namely to go from bad to wore. Disgraceful as the above attempted explanation, made by R. Dubs and John Schneider, was, its worst feature was that it was a *deliberate falsehood*.

The lost letter written by Schneider to Dubs had been written on Nov. 8th, 1877. The letter written by Rev. A. Halmhuber, a part of which Bishop Esher read to Dubs and Heyl, while on a friendly visit at the Bishop's house, was dated Nov. 19th, 1877, and written in Yokohama, Japan, 7000 miles distant! The reading of this letter to Dubs and Heyl occurred on Dec. 20th, 1877, about a month and a half after Schneider wrote his slanderous letter to Dubs! Consequently neither of them knew a single word about that letter until long afterwards, and now they come to Bishop Esher and attempt to cover up their iniquity by a deliberate falsehood. Together they concoct the scheme, and R. Dubs, a bishop of the Evangelical Association, being the more glib tongued of the two conspirators, agrees to tell the lie, and John Schneider, a presiding elder of the Illinois Conference, stands by and corroborates it! And these two men were the principal witnesses in the so-called trials in Chicago and Reading! The entire affair is so wicked and abhorrent that the language with which properly to characterize it might be considered out of place in a book of this kind. Moreover it is such a humiliation for our beloved Church that only the dire necessity, that at last the real inwardness of the wicked rebellion should be known, justifies the writer in presenting these sad facts. No wonder we have been reaping such bitter fruit. What else could the harvest have been with such a man in the highest office in the gift of the Church, and no wonder the results in Illinois were as they were, with such men as John Schneider and Wm. Huelster as presiding elders.

In order to bring out the facts more fully it may be necessary to return to the affairs of the U. B. Institute in their earlier stages.

At first when the difficulties arose Prof. H. H. Rassweiler and Rev. E. L. Kiplinger, the latter the representative of the Indiana Conference in the Trustee Board, both took a very decided stand against the intrigues of the Treasurer, William Huelster. Prof. Rassweiler had no confidence whatever in Huelster's honesty and integrity and frankly said so upon more than one occasion. At one of the meetings of the Board, held with closed doors, Kiplinger mercilessly scored Huelster for his crookedness. Afterwards, when Esher was to be put down, as history frequently repeats itself, these three became firm friends. How the Treasurer, Wm. Huelster, was fulfilling his part in the conspiracy the following extracts from his letters will show. The reader will notice that the dates which are given correspond with the date of Schneider's "lost letter" to Dubs, only a year after Dubs' election as bishop.

On August 12th, 1876, Wm. Huelster in writing to the Secretary of the Board said : "Bishop Esher is seeking his own personal interests and desires to have his son-in-law appointed teacher in the Institute." In another letter, dated Nov. 1st, 1876, written to the same person Huelster says: "Bishop Esher is acting contrary to or against all arrangements of General Conference and the Board of Trustees, and the Bishop's actions mean nothing less than to give the U. B. Institute the deathblow, wherefore the Executive Committee and the treasurer may possibly call an extra session of the Board." Under date of Nov. 9th, 1876, Huelster wrote another letter to the same person in which he brands Bishop Esher "as a deceitful and malicious church politician" and adds, "deplorable as it may seem, this highest officer in our Church must be exposed." These letters are written respectively Aug. 12th, 1876, Nov. 1st, 1876, and Nov. 9th, 1876, and John Schneider's letter to Dubs, Nov. 8th, 1876. Does the reader desire any stronger evidence of the conspiracy? These letters were written to one of the most influential members of the Trustee Board, who was acting as its secretary, and is now the President of the Board of Trustees of N. W. College, Rev. M. Pfitzinger. They were certainly not written without a purpose. To how many more of the Trustees did Huelster write thus? The purpose of these letters will presently appear.

On Dec. 7th, 1878, William Huelster wrote another letter to the same person in which occurs the following: "The Principal does not act, *and he does not resign*. I cannot write you all, but you shall hear it when you get here." On April 12th, 1877 Huelster again wrote the Secretary as follows: "As concerns the formal opening of the Institute I would simply, were I the Executive Committee, fix the time, and invite the Principal to be present and conduct the ceremonies, and if he should refuse to do so I would appoint some one else." The next letter from which an extract is quoted bears date, June 1st, 1877, about a month and a half after the conference session in Washington, Ill., with which the reader is now familiar, and where Bishop Dubs had delivered his "masterpiece" against

Bishop Esher: "If upon those transactions" (meaning the actions of R. Dubs and the Illinois Conference), "*Esher will not resign as Principal*, then an extra session may be necessary, and I would favor such, for then the Board will have to make arrangements in the interests of the Institute. If this is not the case, and if what occurred at our conference is to be investigated, I cannot comprehend how we officers have any right to call an extra session of the Board at an expense of about $150.00, to look into personal matters, and more especially not *in the absence of the person playing the principal part therein*."

Previous to the conference session in Washington, Ill., the Principal, Bishop Esher, was charged with acting contrary to the arrangements of General Conference, and that his actions meant nothing less than to give the U. B. Institute the "death blow." Bishop Dubs in Washington, Ill., just a short time after that appealed to the conference, to take a firm stand in behalf of the Institute which Bishop Esher was about to crush, and the very existence of which he had endangered by his course. Now, a few months later, when the Board is to meet, the only body having authority to act in matters appertaining to the Institute, to inquire into these serious charges which Huelster, Schneider and Dubs had made against the Principal, the matters at issue are only "personal" and not worth even the expenditure of $150.00. On the 28th of March, 1877, the Executive Committee of which John Schneider was a member, passed a resolution calling for an extra session of the Board, and ordered the Treasurer to forward copies to the President and Secretary for their concurrence. The President, Bishop Esher, was more than willing to have an extra session, but Rev. M. Pfitzinger, the secretary, hesitated for some time before giving his consent. Meanwhile, and before the extra session was called, the Illinois Conference had its session at Washington, Ill., April 12, 1877, at which the proceedings against Bishop Esher were taken. Immediately after this conference session was over, namely on the 18th of April, the Executive Committee met, and countermanded the extra session it had ordered on March 28. The "great Illinois Conference had spoken," had adjudged the issues in the absence of the Principal, and had acted for the Trustee Board, and now of course no further action is necessary. The Institution is now no longer endangered! Their resolutions censuring the absent Principal had saved it! There was no further use for a trustee board, nor was it, in the estimation of these parties of any account what the other six or seven annual conferences, all equally interested and all equally responsible, might have to say. R. Dubs, John Schneider, Henry Rohland, W. Huelster and D. B. Byers had passed upon the question, and hence it was settled!

However, the Secretary of the Board, Rev. M. Pfitzinger, who had previously been quite favorably disposed towards Huelster as Huelster's letters show, became convinced through the political manœuvering of Schneider and Huelster that there was something behind the scenes which ought to be exposed, ordered an extra session of the Board. But even after the Secretary had sent the notice to Cleveland for publication these men sent a telegram to the editors countermanding its publication. Why? Simply because in the first place they wanted no investigation. They very well knew that they had duped the Illinois Conference by false testimony which would be exposed at the meeting of the Trustee Board. In the second place, they wanted no investigation, *because they had been after a resignation.* The Executive Committee kept a man in the Institute charged with immorality in the hope they could force Bishop Esher to resign. This failing, then by writing letters to the Trustees undermining his character and charging him with attempting to ruin the Institute, they hoped to gain enough Trustees to compel his resignation. Then, however, the grand opportunity came to them at the Illinois Conference session, and they passed their resolutions of censure, fully expecting by preventing a meeting of the Board of Trustees, to secure the coveted prize in the resignation of Bishop Esher as Principal.

William Huelster himself, in his letter to Rev. M. Pfitzinger, acknowledged this to have been the purpose of the proceedings in Washington, Ill. Rev. M. Pfitzinger did the Church and the cause of truth noble service in ordering that extra session of the Board, as he also did on other occasions during the severe trials through which our Church has passed.

But who was "the absent person playing the principal part herein" spoken of in one of Huelster's letters? And who was the "somebody else" who was to be put into Bishop Esher's place if he could be driven to resign? Bishop Rudolph Dubs was "the person playing the principal part" at Washington, Ill., and Bishop Rudolph Dubs had left for Europe on the 8th day May in that same eventful year, consequently he, according to the admission of one of his co-conspirators, was "the absent person playing the principal part herein." And the "principal part" of the uprising of Dubs at Washington, Ill., was the conspiracy into which he had entered "to put Esher down," and if his resignation as Principal of the Institute could have been secured, it was hoped by these wire-pullers that Rudolph Dubs would be elected Principal of the U. B. Institute, and thus a long step would have been taken towards the goal of their desires and the purpose of their conspiracy.

Before closing this chapter the writer feels that he should again refer to the unbiblical and undisciplinary course pursued by Bishop Dubs at the conference session in Washington, Ill. Bishop Esher's position and opinion on the questions at issue in reference to the manner of proceedure at our College and Institute, located at Naperville, Ill., were well known. It was also well known how much interest he had always manifested in the interests of those institutions. Had he not aided in laying the foundation for those institutions of learning and exerted his personal and official influence in their behalf whenever and wherever an opportunity was found? His opinions differed from those of the Executive Committee, and this fact was known to Bishop Dubs previous to the session of the Illinois

Conference, the differences having been discussed in our church papers. Why, if Bishop Dubs considered Bishop Esher's position and opinion so dangerous to the welfare of the Institute, did he not first at least attempt in a manly and brotherly way if possible to reconcile differences and adjust existing difficulties? Why not first discuss these questions with the Principal of the Institute, who was also Dubs' senior in office? Here would have been an opportunity for "arbitration." Why was Dubs so utterly unwilling to adopt "arbitration" before he made his formal declaration of war at Washington, Ill.? Why not reason together then? Why was no forbearance or charity shown then towards a man whose opinion differed from that of Dubs, and Schneider and Huelster? It was certainly only a matter of opinion. Does not the U. B. Institute still exist notwithstanding these differences of opinion?

However, instead of making a single effort to restore harmony, or "arbitrate" the pending difficulties, Bishop Dubs delivers his great speech in which he assails the motives and official acts of his collegue, and excites the conference in a very unbecoming manner, in fact under the circumstances, in an absolutely unchristian manner, as he had never spoken a word privately with his colleague about the matter, as the Word of God and the Discipline directs. By that speech the seeds of dissension were not only sown deep into the Illinois Conference, but scattered broadcast throughout the entire Church. The harvest has been very plentiful indeed in discord, in rebellion, disruption, and secession.

Instead of pouring oil on the troubled waters in the Illinois Conference, Bishop Dubs threw the firebrand in the shape of his "masterpiece" into the inflammable material of the Illinois Conference, and from thence the fire spread through the Church, and has been raging since. It has consumed Dubs himself as well as a large portion of the Illinois Conference, and his followers elsewhere. Eternity alone will reveal the fearful extent of the harm done. The only comfort in connection with the sad history is that it has also to a great extent proved to be a fire of cleansing, consuming the dross, and that the pure gold will only become more purified.

CHAPTER III.

The Ecumenical Conference Affair.

At the General Conference in 1879 an invitation was received to co-operate in the holding of an Ecumenical Conference of Methodistic bodies for the discussion of subjects common to Methodism. This invitation was accepted and a committee appointed to co-operate with the various committees of Methodistic bodies throughout the world in order to make the necessary preliminary arrangements. Bishop R. Dubs and Rev. D. B. Byers were appointed as such committee. At the time this invitation was extended and accepted it could not as yet be known whether such a conference would be held. That was dependent upon whether or not the project would find favor with the various Methodistic churches or not. Hence no basis of representation had as yet been fixed, and the General Conference could not elect delegates to represent our Church in the Ecumenical Conference. Nevertheless, Dubs and Byers set up the absurd claim that they were not only to represent our Church in the committee of correspondence as it was termed, but also as the delegates from our Church to the Ecumenical Conference. Their claim to such an appointment, however, was not recognized at any time by the Board of Bishops, by the officials at Cleveland, or by the Church in any official capacity.

At a meeting of the Board of Bishops held in Cleveland, O., Oct. 5th, 1880, delegates to the Ecumenical Conference were elected. Bishop Dubs, the secretary of the Board, officially published the action of the Bishops in the following manner: "The attendance upon the Ecumenical Council of the Methodist

Churches and Associations was also discussed. Our Association is entitled to six delegates. Bishop Dubs and Rev. D. B. Byers were appointed by General Conference as delegates, and to these the Bishops now added Bishop Bowman and Rev. H. Hintze of the Germany Conference. Bro. Hintze appointed in North Germany, has but a comparatively short distance to travel to England, and is conversant with the English language." As soon as this report had been published, Bishop Esher immediately called Bishop Dubs' attention to its incorrectness. Bishop Dubs had published as our official secretary *what was merely his own personal opinion as the action of the Bishops.* That "Bishop Dubs and Rev. D. B. Byers were appointed by General Conference as delegates" was not even "discussed" in the official proceedings of the Board of Bishops, much less agreed upon. Hence the statement made by Bishop Dubs that "to these the Bishops now added Bishop Bowman and Rev. H. Hintze" was also incorrect and misleading. These two had been appointed by the Bishops without any reference to any previous appointment. Bishop Dubs knew when he thus incorrectly published our proceedings that he was willfully, and for his own selfish purposes officially falsifying the record. Nor did he ever correct his falsification, and for the sake of peace we allowed it to stand.

Under date of March 16th, 1881 Dubs wrote the following letter to Rev. Dr. A. C. George, the Secretary of the Ecumenical Conference committee.

"Cleveland, O., March 16, 1881.

Rev. Dr. George

My dear Sir: It seems Bishop Esher informed you, that our General Conference elected no delegates to the great Methodist Council. Please read on Page 67, 90 and 93 in our Gen. Conf. Journal I send you to-day. Bishop Esher's course is *surprising* and *astonishing.* I will not explain this matter to you. Your committee (see page 29) may have been preliminary; ours is for Council and preparatory matters.

It may be, that our General Conference would have acted somewhat different, if it had been known that the Council would be of such magnitude, and be in London, but that does not invalidate Rev. Byers' and my election. I never purposed to go, and Rev. D. B. Byers cannot be kept back. Where does Bishop Esher get power to appoint delegates? Our General Conference did not say one single word that the Bishop should appoint them. At an Episcopal meeting he suggested that Bishop Bowman ought to be appointed and Bro. Hintze from Germany and I did say yes, as I had not given the matter any thought. But now I have looked up the matter and see clearly, that Esher's and my action in the case of Bishop Bowman and Hintze is illegal, if anything in connection with this matter is to be considered thus.

Very respectfully yours
R. Dubs, Bishop of Evangelical Association.
Residence 55 Beech St., Cleveland, Ohio."

This copy of the original letter is sworn to by the person who made it, and is further certified by two witnesses who compared the copy with the original.

The reader has seen how Bishop Dubs at Washington, Ill., publicly and officially assailed his colleague, Bishop Esher, and has also been furnished with the evidence that there was no foundation in fact for the serious charges he made against his colleague, and that Bishop Dubs had made this public attack without having previously said a word about the matter to Bishop Esher, and without the least attempt to adjust existing differences. Now it will be seen the same course is pursued again, only that now, after first officially falsifying the records of the Board, and thereby placing his colleagues in an entirely wrong light before the Church, he assails both of his colleagues officially by signing himself as "Bishop of the Evangelical Association". Nor does he, in this very remarkable letter, assail merely us personally, but assails the action of the Board of Bishops, declaring the same to have been "illegal", and the action taken having been unauthorized. Why not before he thus officially assails his colleagues, and casts such undeserved reflections upon their official integrity, and even upon their intelligence in a letter to a minister of another Church, at least mention the matter to them? Differences of opinion existed, why not at least attempt to "arbitrate" them before entering his official protest against the seats of the delegates appointed bo the Board of Bishops, the appointment of which he himself had officially published in our church papers? Bishop Dubs did not even have the manliness and courage to inform either Rev. H. Hintze or the writer that he had protested against our admission as delegates from our Church. The whole thing was done in a stealthy and cowardly manner, and only discovered through the frankness and brotherly consideration of Dr. George, whose indignation had been aroused by Bishop Dubs' treachery and disrespect toward his colleagues. Had Dubs succeeded in his plans the disgrace of having been refused seats in that honorable body would have been fastened upon us personally, and upon our Church. He could have no other purpose in view. Some of his friends it seemed expected he would succeed, as Rev. S. Neitz afterwards expressed great surprise to the writer that our delegates had been given seats. Rudolph Dubs' treachery and cowardice are manifest at every step in this sad history.

The worst, however, in connection with this letter to Dr. George, in which Bishop Dubs so seriously attacks his colleagues, remains to be written. That entire letter to Dr. George signed by "R. Dubs, Bishop of the Evangelical Association" is a deliberate falsification from beginning to end, and was written with the intent to misrepresent and deceive. In it he says that at the time of the Episcopal meeting when Bro. Hintze and Bishop Bowman were appointed he "had not given the matter any thought". And yet before that meeting was held he called the writer of this volume aside in the Publishing House in Cleveland, O., and called his attention to the paragraphs in the General Conference journal bearing upon the question, and tried his utmost to convince him that himself (Dubs) and Rev. D. B. Byers had been elected not only as our representatives on the committee of correspondence, but also as delegates to the Council. Moreover when the episcopal Board was in session, and Dubs introduced the appointment of delegates to the Conference in London, and Bishop Esher raised the question whether the Board of Bishops was authorized to make the appointment, he was ready with arguments to prove that there was no question whatever about the authority of the episcopal Board to act. These two things show that he had given the matter much thought and that he was deeply interested. Hence this was falsehood number one in this official letter. Further on in this very remarkable letter signed "R. Dubs, Bishop of the Evangelical Association" its author says: "Where does Bishop Esher get the power to appoint delegates?" And yet this same Rudolph Dubs and the same Bishop had published as the reader has seen, over his own signature in his official capacity, that the Board of Bishops had appointed delegates! Hence this was falsehood number two. Further on this same "R. Dubs, Bishop" etc. says: "At an Episcopal meeting he (Bishop Esher) suggested that Bishop Bowman ought to be appointed, and Bro. Hintze from Germany, and I did say yes." This was falsehood number three. It was in fact such a deliberate wilful falsification that the shorter and more expressive anglo-saxon term ought to be used. Presume when he penned this official letter to Dr. George he had no idea it would ever see the light of day, which makes it all the worse, and the sin so much greater. "R. Dubs, Bishop" etc. will be convicted of deliberately writing the untruth to Dr. George by the evidence of Bishop R. Dubs himself. In an article published in the *Evangelical Messenger*, under date of Nov. 22, 1881, signed by R. Dubs, appears the following paragraph: "Bishop Esher has again called attention to the part I took in the appointment of Bishop Bowman and Rev. H. Hintze as additional delegates to the Ecumenical Conference. I will explain how it came to pass. Bishop Bowman asked me whether I would go to London. I said I would not, but since he was to go to Europe, and we were entitled to six delegates, I thought he ought to be one of them. The matter was discussed in an official meeting and Bishop Esher being chairman of the Board of Bishops, and Bishop Bowman being personally interested, the latter would not, of course, move his own appointment, therefore it was perfectly natural that I should make the motion to appoint him. Any different construction put on my action is misleading and incorrect." Under date of March 16, 1891 in a letter to Dr. George the secretary of the Ecumenical Conference, "R. Dubs, Bishop," etc. writes, " where does Bishop Esher get the power to appoint delegates," " he (Bishop Esher) suggested that Bishop Bowman ought to be appointed and Bro. Hintze from Germany and I did say yes." Under date of Nov. 22, 1881, R. Dubs writes, " it was perfectly natural that I should make the motion to appoint him," namely Bishop Bowman. In the article quoted above Bishop Dubs did not tell the whole truth. He also moved that Bro. Hintze should be appointed and Bishop Bowman seconded the motion, so that in reality Bishop Esher had nothing more to do than give his assent. And this was all he had done in the appointment of Bishop Bowman. Bishop R. Dubs had managed the whole affair, and in the opinion of the writer for no other purpose than that he hoped thereby to win him over to his view of the action of the General Conference, so his friend and fellow helper in the cause of the " minority " could go to London. He had been successful with others by the use of such means and hoped thereby to flatter the writer so as to use him for his purposes.

" But," probably some one may say, " why did Bishops Esher and Bowman keep silent, knowing these facts ? " *They did not.* They informed the Church of the misdeeds of Bishop R. Dubs. Soon after these sad facts came to our knowledge an official meeting was held at which nearly if not quite all the general officers of the Church were present, and also several others of our leading ministers, in all at least a dozen if not more preachers. This meeting was held in the Publishing House at Cleveland, O. After the regular business of the meeting had been disposed of, Bishop Esher arose and in plain and unequivocal language charged Bishop R. Dubs with having written a wilful deliberate falsehood. He spoke in German. The language he used was: *Bischof Dubs hat die Unwahrheit geschrieben, und er hat gewusst, wie er es geschrieben hat, dass es die Unwahrheit ist.* ("Bishop Dubs wrote the untruth, and he knew when he wrote it that it was untrue.") Bishop Bowman corroborated Bishop Esher's statements. This was done in the hope that Dubs would not allow such a direct charge of immorality to be made against him, without demanding the evidence; or, if he would do so, the ministers present would demand an examination into the matter at once. We were disappointed. Bishop Dubs went away from the meeting and continued as before, with the charge of falsehood standing against him deliberately made by his colleagues, and the other ministers, for peace's sake, or some other unexplained reason, did the same thing. At the General Conference in Allentown, Pa., both Bishop Esher and Bishop Bowman reiterated their accusations of falsehoood on the part of Bishop Dubs. But the friends of Dubs wanted no investigation into the facts; they were only anxious for peace—for peace almost at any price. Unfortunately the Church yielded. The price has since been paid.

However, in order to bring out the true inwardness of this sad affair something more need be said. In several articles written by Bishop Dubs, in the Fall of 1881, for the *Evangelical Messenger*, he tried to make it appear that Bishop Bowman agreed with him in his views in reference to the theory that the General Conference in Chicago had elected delegates to the Ecumenical Conference. Hence under date of Dec. 16, 1881, Bishop Bowman replied to these articles, from which the following quotation is made: "Whereas I also have been dragged into the unprofitable controversy about the Ecumenical Conference delegate question, I am compelled to say a few words, although I do so very reluctantly for obvious reasons. I shall say a few words only; first, because I have no desire to enter into details, and shall not unless *compelled* to do so. Secondly, because my physician has *commanded* physical and mental rest, and I am even now violating his directions. Suffice it then to say, that if Bishop Dubs believes that I, *at any time*, entertained the absurd idea that our General Conference had elected delegates to the Ecumenical Conference, he is simply mistaken. I will also add that Bro. Hintze and myself were not appointed 'additional' delegates. The term 'additional' was not in either of the motions by which we were appointed. I, of course, voted along with my colleagues in the appointment of Bro. Hintze, which I certainly would not have done had 'additional' been in the wording of the resolution.

"The veracity of a Bishop of the Evangelical Association was involved, hence I publicly write Bishop Dubs was 'mistaken.' Privately, however, I could not conscientiously allow such deliberate falsehoods on the part of a minister and Bishop of our Church to pass by unrebuked, and as I was at the time physically unable to write, having been prostrated by a spinal injury received by a fall on ship-board on my return trip from Europe, I dictated the following letter to my daughter, of which a copy was also sent to Bishop Esher:

"Allentown, Nov. 25, 1881.

"*Bro. Dubs:*—I have just read your remarkable article in the *Messenger* entitled "My Answer." I was scarcely able to believe my own eyes, and yet there it stands black on white. In the first place it is very unkind and unbrotherly, yea, even cruel to drag a brother who is lying on his bed of affliction and pain, not even able to write a sentence himself, into such a controversy in order to help yourself out of an unpleasant dilemma, into which you brought yourself by your own actions. However, this is not the worst. Your present article is a flat contradiction of the statements made in a former article, and what is even still worse, you make statements which are not true. I never asked you whether you would go to London. Secondly, you know that your first statement in your second paragraph in which you speak of the majority of the bishops at their official meeting is also untrue. Excuse me for using such plain language. The other matters of which you speak do not concern me personally, and upon them I have nothing to say. But is it not a shame and an outrage to force me into the unpleasant position of either standing misrepresented before the Church, or compel me publicly to say that what you have written is not true?

"Yours in sorrow
"Thomas Bowman.
"per L. L. B."

In this matter Bishop Dubs adopted his usual course of being silent when confronted with his wrong-doing, and when he knew he could not controvert the facts and the evidence. He made no reply to the article in the *Messenger*, because he knew then the facts would be stated and he would be proven to have been a falsifier. Nor did he ever reply to the letter in which Bishop Bowman, through his daughter, accused him of falsehood, and he knew that a copy of the same had been sent to Bishop Esher. Several months later he called at the writer's home in Allentown, Pa., in company with one of his lieutenants, for the purpose, as the writer expected, of talking the matter over, and if possible, adjusting things, but he left again, without so much as mentioning it. Why? Was Dubs ever backward in his defence when it was possible to defend himself? His entire history fully answers the question. The policy of silence was only adopted when he knew the facts were against him, and when a defence on his part would but bring out his crimes in more startling features. The only time he ventured to depart from this policy, was when he undertook to defend the course, he pursued in Europe, in reference to their delegations to the General Conference of 1887.

CHAPTER IV.

Clewell for Assistant Editor of the "Messenger."

Just previous to and during the General Conference of 1879, it was whispered in confidential circles that in the event of Rev. H. B. Hartzler's election as Editor of the *Evangelical Messenger*, T. G. Clewell, a former editor, was to be appointed Hartzler's assistant. This Clewell was the editor, who years ago resigned while charges of heresy were pending against him. Before doing so, he made an attempt, through the civil courts, to have the Board of Publication enjoined from acting upon the charges. He has the distinction (?) of being the first minister of our Church who dragged the Church into the civil court in order to present an adjudiction of ecclesiastical questions in accordance with the Discipline. After an inglorious defeat in the court, to which he had appealed, he resigned his office, well knowing that the evidence against him was overwhelming. The "Dubs party" or "minority," heretofore mentioned, whose intrigue could be plainly seen in the proceedings of the General Conference of 1879, after the conference had adjourned, set about circulating petitions, etc., for the purpose of creating sentiment in favor of Clewell's appointment, more especially also in order to offer some sort of excuse for his appointment, which had been determined upon by the leaders of the Dubs faction before the General Conference of 1879 had closed. The law of the Church at that time was that the appointment of the assistant needed only the confirmation of the Executive Committee of the Board of Publication. This committee consisted of R. Dubs, Revs. W. W. Orwig and Chas Hammer. The last two were by this time quite advanced in years, and not inclined to offer much resistance to anything, least of all the plans of a bishop of the Church. Those who were employed in the Publishing House at that time, as well as the Publishers, could testify how Dubs lorded it over these two brethren when together in Executive Committee session.* He was to all intents and purposes the Executive Committee of those days. This had also been the case during the first four years of his episcopal term, when he was the only one of the bishops who was a member of the Board of Publication, coercing every one into doing his bidding. No man in the history of our Church ever ruled with such despotic power as did Bishop Rudolph Dubs in the first term of his episcopal office. This was not only the case in Cleveland at the Publishing House, but in the Annual Conferences as well. Even Rev. S. Neitz designated him the "German Pope" (*der deutsche Papst*) during the first session of the East Pa. Conference, at which he presided, because he so unmercifully lorded it over several brethren of the conference. Hence as he was the controlling power of affairs in Cleveland, Ohio, at that time the responsibility for the appointment of T. G. Clewell as assistant editor of the *Evangelical Messenger*, one of the greatest outrages ever perpetrated upon the Church by General Conference officers, rests with Rudolph Dubs and H. B. Hartzler, two of the most erratic men ever elected to office in our Church.

Clewell was received into the Church by the East Pa. Conference at its session in Weissport, Pa., in the last week of

---

* A spicy sample of business of the Ex. Committee was one day wittnessed by the undersigned, when he happened to enter the room where the meeting was held. Dubs had just introduced a certain subject and impressed its importance with all the eloquence of his words and motions upon the two old gentlemen and concluded by saying in a commanding tone: "Thus we will fix it, will we not Father Orwig? put it down Brother Hammer!"—Without motion, without debate and without voting upon the subject. The chief had spoken, that settled the matter.

W. H.

February, 1880, after he had already been appointed and confirmed as assistant editor in January previous, hence the Church had an assistant editor of one of its official papers for nearly two months who was not a member nor minister of our Church, who had formerly withdrawn under charges of heresy, and had not in the least changed his views, or ever apologized for sending the sheriff upon the officers of the Church. This scheme was manipulated by a Bishop of the Church in order to get an able lieutenant to aid him in his conspiracy against his senior in office, who, according to his way of thinking, was the *one* man in his way towards assuming complete personal control of the Church!

Rev. C. Hammer it seems after all offered some opposition to the appointment of Clewell. It therefore became necessary to overcome his convictions of propriety. Dubs, however, was equal to the emergency. Rev. S. Neitz was at that time a member of the Board of Publication, representing the East Pa. Conference; he was also a brother in-law of Rev. C. Hammer, hence had considerable personal and official influence with the latter. Dubs knew that Neitz would only be too glad to have his old ally in his fight against the doctrine of entire sanctification back in an official position. He knew also that he would be an able helper to "put down" the man who had been elected bishop over him, so that Dubs knew that his "friend Neitz" would be ready to lend a helping hand, not because he had any personal respect for Dubs, or had any use for him further, than as an instrument to gratify his own personal feelings. (To at least two living witnesses Neitz had declared Dubs guilty of falsehood and deception.)

So Dubs wrote Neitz that he should at once write to Bro. Hammer and use his influence with him to vote for Clewell's confirmation. His letter had made some impression upon Bro. Hammer, so Dubs writes to Neitz requesting him to write again, which he did. In this way Bro. Hammer was persuaded. The evidence to prove these things is at hand. However, that

Clewell at the time of his appointment was not a minister of our Church, that he had been guilty of transgressing a plain provision of our discipline, punishable by expulsion, and that he was not in harmony either with our doctrine or church polity, nor with the genius of our Association, were not the worst features of the appointment, although certainly injurious enough. We add a copy of a letter written by one of the oldest as well as ablest ministers of the Ohio Conference at that time in reply to certain questions addressed to him by another minister of our Church. The name of the writer is withheld for prudential reasons, the original, however, is in the writer's possession and can be produced whenever it may become necessary.

The letter, dated April, 18, 1882, reads as follows:

"Dear Brother!—You ask me why the Ohio Conference rejected Clewell and his credentials. This is a double question. I will endeavor to answer it. The reason we would not receive *him* is because we did not want him, and the reason we did not want him, is because we did not believe in his piety, nor true loyalty to the Church, and that which brought us to this conclusion, was his conduct which led to his deposition from the editorship of the *Messenger*, and we were strengthened in this opinion by what R. Dubs and others told us about him after the Pittsburg Conference session, in which Dubs took such an active part, had ratified the proceedings of the Board of Publication in Clewell's case, he (Dubs) talked to me and other members of the Ohio Conference quite freely about the matter. He then said there had been a conspiracy by Clewell and some of his friends in the Pittsburg Conference, plotting against the Church, and by exposing this plot he succeeded in arraying Clewell and his friends against each other and by this means led the conference to ratify the action of the Board. Dubs also told me and other members of the conference that he had no doubt Clewell was guilty of adultery. These were some of the things which led us to distrust the man, and some of the reasons why we did not want him as a member of our conference. Now under these circumstances Clewell left our Church, and got back again without ever making any confession of his wrongs, but on the contrary justifies all he did except the act of sending the sheriff to the Board and serving an injunction on its proceedings, and this he politely charges to the wrong advice of his friends. The reason we rejected Clewell's credentials is because we believe them to be illegal on the ground:

(1) The license which he held from the M. E. Church, and by which he united with the East Pa. Conference was dead, not having been renewed at the proper time.

(2) Because our Book of Discipline says that a preacher in our Church cannot be a member of one Annual Conference, and live within the bounds of another conference, so we also hold that it is unlawful for a conference to receive a man as a preacher who lives within the bounds of another Annual Conference, hence we regard the reception of Clewell by the East Pa. Conference illegal, and that he could not by an unlawful act be received into legal relations, and on this ground we hold that the credentials given him by the East Pa. Conference and presented to us were not valid, and hence the rejection. I also believe that the whole Clewell affair is a part of a scheme of a party in our Church for a purpose. Rule or ruin seems to be the object."

In order to corroborate this brother in his main statement extracts will also be cited from an editorial in the *Christliche Botschafter*, the German official organ of our Church, under date of April 5, 1871, written by Rudolph Dubs, who was then its editor, in reply to an article written by Rev. S. G. Rhoads of the East Pa. Conference. Dubs says: " In this number our readers will find an article from the pen of Bro. S. G. Rhoads whose name is found attached to the majority report of the East Pa. Conference, and therefore feels himself called to defend the action of the East Pa. Conference which has defended Brother Clewell's *revolutionary actions.*" Further on in the same editorial speaking of the action of the East Pa. Conference in the Clewell case, Dubs says: "They must now defend at the General Conference the fact that Clewell's *outrage upon our articles of faith, this revolutionary attack upon the foundation of our Church was essentially correct.*" "Can Bro. Rhoads quote a Methodist paper in which attacks are made upon their articles of faith, as they were made by Clewell upon ours? No Editor of the M. E. Church would make himself guilty of such an ecclesiastical crime; they love the foundations of the faith of their Church to much."

Thus R. Dubs wrote of the man he afterwards forced into the position of assistant to the Editor of our English Church organ in order to aid him in a conspiracy into which he had entered. Moreover, what he had written about Clewell, although it contained fearful charges, was after all not as bad as what he had said about him, as the above letter proves. And the writer of that letter does notst and alone. His statements can be corroborated by others to whom Dubs said the same thing. Dubs even went so far as to say that while living a near neighbor to Clewell on Harmon Street in Cleveland, O., he was compelled to go into Clewell's family and make peace on account of the jealousy caused by the fearful crime with which he had charged Clewell.

Here, indeed, is a spectacle. A Bishop of the Church is " to take care that everything be done according to the Word of God, to watch faithfully over the flock of Christ, feeding them with wholesome doctrine, and guiding them with strict discipline." This Bishop, however, having an "India Rubber conscience," and having turned church politician, pulls the wires so as to put a known advocate of unsound doctrine into a position of vast influence over the entire flock, whom Dubs had charged, in the official papers of the Church of which he was Editor at the time, of being guilty of "revolutionary actions," of an "outrage upon our articles of faith," of a " revolutionary attack upon the foundation of our Church, and of an ecclesiastical crime "; a man guilty of dragging his own Church before the civil courts, and what is worse than all a man who Dubs says was "guilty of adultery." Of the truth of this latter fearful charge the writer knows nothing, and most sincerely hopes it is not true. In fact as Dubs' reputation for slander and falsehood could not well be worse, the writer is disinclined to believe this accusation upon the assertion of Dubs alone. Dubs, however, has made it, and if it is not true it brands him as a slanderer and the author of a falsehood ; and if it should be true it brands him as a corrupt and wicked man who would stoop to any means by which to conquer, and carry out his ends. What else could the harvest have been but dissension and schism ?

Very soon after Clewell had been installed, the "Association" idea was advanced in the *Evangelical Messenger* and carried to such extremes that the term "Church" as applied to the Evangelical Association was not at all used in its columns. If correspondents used the term "Church" in connection with our Church, it was always changed into "Association" by the editors. Even if our ministers in obituary notices would say "deceased was a member of our Church," the editors would make them say "a member of our Association." Until finally one could only read "our Association" and "our Association" and preachers and people became disgusted. The purpose of this was to create a sentiment of opposition against strict discipline in the general affairs of the Church. The party represented by Dubs, Hartzler and Clewell then already attempted to invest the Annual Conferences with supreme authority, and to make the impression that the various Boards of the Church, the Bishops, and the General Conference, were invested with no authority, hence had no jurisdiction to discipline the general officers of the Church, as we were "merely an Association."

This was the position assumed by S. Neitz at the General Conference in 1859 in Naperville, Ill., when charges were preferred against him. This was the position assumed by H. B. Hartzler when charges were preferred against him at the General Conference at Buffalo, N. Y., in 1887. The plan of the Dubs' faction at this latter General Conference in Buffalo was, to enter a protest against the proceedings in the Hartzler case, then leave the conference room in a body, and by so doing break the quorum. C. S. Haman was to take the lead in this treasonable act, but his courage failed him when the time for action came.

The author of this work in an article in the *Evangelical Messenger* called attention to the position the *Messenger* assumed, showing that its teachings were at variance with our discipline, and its results injurious to the Church. For publishing this article he was assailed by the editor and his assistant with all the acrimony of which they were capable. And as usual with the faction, in order in their minds to strengthen a weak cause, they made some ugly insinuations against the writer's character. This resulted in formal charges against the editor. But when the Board of Publication convened H. B. Hartzler *was not ready for trial.* Hence an extra session of the Board would have been necessary, connected with much expense and loss of time. The editor then offered to withdraw the insinuations he had made, and so the matter was dropped and compromised. Had he then been dealt with as he so richly deserved, he would not have had so great an opportunity to sow the seeds of dissension as he did. While Clewell was editor in chief he was content with " a revolutionary attack upon the foundation of our Church," but when assistant to Hartzler these two conspired together to set the Church aside altogether, so that the fullest license might be enjoyed and every one be permitted to do as seemed good in his sight.

The doctrine of State Rights as taught in the South, and held by many in the North, plunged this fair country into a civil war which cost millions of dollars and thousands of human lives, with all the suffering incident to war. The doctrine of Conference Rights as taught for the past generation especially in the East, aided materially in destroying the unity of our Church, and culminated in the meeting of its adherents in Philadelphia, in setting up a rump conference in direct opposition to the action of the General Conference of the Evangelical Association. To secure the property of the Church against these pretenders has cost thousands of dollars, brought disgrace upon the cause of religion, and it is to be feared will result in the ruin of many precious souls for whom Christ died.

CHAPTER V.

Efforts looking towards an amicable adjustment of the Difficulties.

THE FIRST ATTEMPT AT ADJUSTMENT.

At a meeting of the Bishops held in Buffalo, N. Y., in connection with a meeting of the Board of Missions, the matters connected with the U. B. Institute were discussed, and it was finally agreed to call a committee to arbitrate and adjust the difficulties if possible. Of this committee, three of the Bishops, namely R. Yeakel, R. Dubs, and Thomas Bowman, were to be members, and these were to choose one additional person. Bishop Esher was to select three persons, and the Executive Committee of the Institute three. The Bishops chose Rev. E. L. Kiplinger. Bishop Esher selected Revs. C. Hummel, M. Pfitzinger, and G. Vetter. The Ex. Committee selected Revs. D. B. Byers, D. Kramer, and C. Lindeman, all of the Illinois Conference, and all of whom had already expressed their opinion by having been in full accord with the resolutions passed by their conference at its session in Washington, Ill. These three with R. Dubs, who had inspired the resolutions adopted at Washington, Ill., were therefore in every respect the allies and partisans of the Executive Committee. When this commission of arbitration met it was agreed, upon Bishop Dubs' persistent arguments, that no personal matters should be introduced, only such things as were connected directly with the affairs of the Institute.

This was a fatal error to begin with. Moreover as R. Dubs was one of the arbitration commission, his personal and official misconduct towards Bishop Esher, and even the things so closely connected with the U. B. Institute proceedings and affairs could not be considered. Hence the most vital points and differences could receive no consideration. It was a "Peace-Committee," hence it was argued everything must be avoided which might in any way disturb the peace of the commission. In view of such a manner of procedure it need not be a matter of surprise that the "peace" it made did not last over night.

When the commission met the writer was elected chairman. He insisted that, as the commission had no judicial functions, and it was optional with either party to accept or reject any conclusions which might be arrived at, some agreement or understanding must be had, before we could proceed. The Executive Committee made no proposition; after repeated declarations by the chairman that the parties should submit some proposition, Bishop Esher made in substance the following statement: "I have already repeatedly offered peacefully to adjust our differences, but my offers were not well received, hence I have no further proposition to make at this time. The other side may make a proposition now. *I desire and demand justice.* I desire peace and rest, but a peace based upon righteousness. I believe in God who loves righteousness, and in the Word of God which teaches that the fruits of righteousness shall be peace. This rest I desire. I want no compromise and shall accept none. I want what is just be it reward or punishment. Investigate my private life for the past forty-five years; investigate my family life, and my official life. Go twenty feet below the surface, and what you may find wrong bring it out, only no compromise. Whereas my friends on the other side have no proposition to offer, I will propose the same basis I have offered on several occasions : If I have erred, or done any wrong, and by so doing have injured any ones' reputation or good name, and it will be shown to me, I will recall what I have said, and right the wrong, as it is right in the sight of God and man, that is as publicly as the mistake was made or the wrong done. The commission of ten shall decide upon the points at issue, and also say in what manner the wrong shall be righted."

After this proposition was made by the Bishop, the Executive Committee, composed of John Schneider, H. Rohland, and Wm. Huelster withdrew to consult, and upon returning delared they would accept the basis laid down by Bishop Esher.

After deliberating upon the matters presented, the following was adopted by the commission:

"1. *Resolved*, That no evidence has been presented to prove that Bishop Esher desired the appointment of his son-in-law.

"2. *Resolved*, That the Executive Committee on account of certain circumstances, as they appeared unto them, had reasons to believe, that Bishop Esher desired the appointment of his son-in-law, hence is not to be censured that it wilfully and knowingly misrepresented the true facts that Bishop Esher did not seek or desire the appointment of his son-in-law.

"3. The figure in the letter so frequently mentioned is plainly to be read as figure one, and ought to have been thus read: Whereas the Executive Committee acknowledges that they were not in the clear about this figure, they should have asked Bishop Esher about it to discover the true meaning. Bishop Esher ought also when the letter was read at the Board meeting, to have corrected the wrong reading. Through his silence the Ex. Committee was strengthened in a mistaken opinion. The Committee cannot be accused of wilfully falsifying.

"4. That we very much regret, that since the Board of Trustees, which acted on these matters, this unfortunate matter was still agitated. This ought not to have been done.

"5. We are of the opinion that Bishop Esher through his actions has not endangered the purity of the Church.

"6. That we request both parties in accordance with these resolutions and declarations to meet each other and lay aside their differences for ever."

This report was written by Bishop Dubs, the man "who played the principal part" in the Institute difficulties, and who was the most deeply interested party of all connected with the sad affair. The report, as the reader cannot help but perceive, completely exonerates Bishop Esher from all the abuse heaped upon him by J. Schneider and W. Huelster, and by R. Dubs himself. According to this report written by Dubs and signed by the three partisans of the U. B. Institute Executive Committee

Bishop Esher was declared innocent of all the fearful accusations which these men, Dubs included, had made against him.

This report further asserts that the letter written by Bishop Esher upon which J. Schneider had circulated the false accusations against the Bishop was so plainly written that no mistake was possible, hence how could it have been read otherwise except by wilful falsification? But something had to be done to white-wash his friends, and also in a manner himself, hence Dubs inserted the "however as it appeared unto them." Bishop Yeakel knew, the author of this volume knew, Revs. M. Pfitzinger, and C. Hummel and G. Vetter knew that this statement was not in accordance with the truth. All of them furthermore knew it had been inserted for the purpose of shielding Dubs' friends. All raised their objections. Dubs, however, pleaded for leniency, for compromise, for peace. "We must have a unanimous report" was his plea. "You must give way in some things, especially as Bishop Esher is so completely exonerated, something must also be done to satisfy the other side."

Finally, persuaded by Dubs' pleadings, the writer, as one of the commission, notwithstanding his convictions that the second and third section in the report were simply an adroit effort on the part of Dubs to extricate himself and his friends, gave way in the delusive hope that probably after all peace might be restored. Presumably this was the case also with others of the commission. Besides at that time neither of us had any conception of the iniquity and treachery of the parties with whom we were dealing. While it was evident that they had done a great wrong, we were nevertheless inclined, in the hope of possible harmony, to cover their sins with the mantle of charity. Especially had no one of us, except possibly the men chosen by the Executive Committee, any idea at that time that Dubs was in league with those parties to the extent he actually was— much less that as his friend Wm. Hueslter had claimed that "he was playing the principal part" in the affair, and yet was one of the arbitrators, and the one who wrote the report.

Every intelligent reader will at once see the error the commission made. Peace can only be lasting or even desirable when founded on truth and righteousness. Everything else is delusive. It can have no permanency, and generally serves only to increase the difficulties. Such was our experience and the outcome of this first attempt at arbitration. Still had it not been for occurrences immediately following, the cobweb which had been woven might perhaps have endured for a while, for it is evident from the spirit of forbearance and charity shown by those members of that peace commission, who were not personally interested in the settlement (as was the case with Dubs, Byers, Kramer and Lindeman), and acted solely, as they believed, in the interests of the Church and of harmony, that they were willing to endure much and go far to accomplish such a desireable end. Bishop Esher manifested the same spirit by accepting a compromise verdict nothwithstanding his previous declaration. But, as the reader is already aware, on that very evening, after this compromise had been made and accepted, and the parties were to come together and lay aside their differences, Rudolph Dubs and John Schneider came to Bishop Esher and again deliberately and wilfully deceived and belied him concerning the intent of the lost letter. At the moment it was done Bishop Esher accepted their dishonorable and certainly for professed ministers of the Gospel, humilating confession, although he could not help being filled with indignation at such ill-bred and reprehensible conduct by men occupying high positions in the church of God. After Bishop Esher returned to his home that evening he informed his wife what the "forschen" (finding out) meant in Schneider's lost letter. Mrs. Esher at once informed her husband that he had been deceived, as she remembered the dates. Hereupon the letter of Bro. Halmhuber, and the date of Bishop Dubs' visit in company with Rev. M. Heyl at Bishop Esher's house, when the Halmhuber letter was read, were looked up, and to their surprise and sorrow the evidence, black on white, about which there could be neither error nor misunderstanding was before them, that Rudolph Dubs and John Schneider had agreed together to go to Bishop Esher and tell him a deliberate falsehood, in order to cover up their iniquity. Moreover soon after this "Peace Meeting" adjourned Dubs said to several brethren in Canada: "Esher is as deep in the mud as the others in the mire," although according to the report which Dubs himself had written, Bishop Esher had been completely exonerated. Is it a wonder, dear reader, that this attempt at arbitration failed so completely?

At the close of this eventful evening when this "Peace Meeting" was held another incident occured which, in connection with the other rumors of Dubs' conduct towards the opposite sex, went far to destroy confidence in the purity of his character. It was after 10 o'clock at night when the meeting adjourned. At this late hour Bishop Dubs was seen to step into a closed carriage, in company with a woman, the wife of another man, with whom, according to the reports circulated, he held a regular correspondence, concerning whose intimacy with Dubs there had been considerable suspicion and talk, and drove to the depot with her alone, a distance of at least two miles. By walking a few blocks he might have reached the depot by using the horse cars. These things are so closely interwoven with the history of these difficulties that the circumstances demand they must be given.

THE SECOND ATTEMPT LOOKING TO ADJUSTMENT.

On the 11th of Oct., 1881, the annual meeting of the bishops was held in Reading, Pa., in the church on 8th Street. After the routine business had been transacted, the writer called the attention of his colleagues to the relations existing between the bishops, and suggested that an earnest effort be made if at all possible to have the difficulties adjusted. In giving the account of this attempt to adjust matters, the writer for the sake of clearness as well as brevity will use the personal pronoun when alluding to himself. Neither of my colleagues seemed to be inclined to make an effort to adjudicate matters. Bishop Esher afterwards assigned as the reason for the course he pursued that he had no faith that anything would be accomplished. Why Bishop Dubs was dis-inclined to make an attempt, I do not know. I, however, insisted with a good deal of earnestness and persistence upon the necessity of at least making an effort, saying, that much harm had already resulted from the condition of things, and that greater injury to the Church would follow if matters could not in some way be adjusted. Still receiving no favorable response from either of my colleagues, I further stated that I had no heart whatever under existing circumstances to go on with my work as one of the bishops, and even went so far as to threaten to resign if no attempt would be made to adjust matters. Finally, Bishop Esher agreed to make an attempt, and Bishop Dubs also at least tacitly consented, though very reluctantly. I then suggested that as Bishop Esher was our senior in office, as well as the oldest in years, he should frankly and plainly state the grievances he might have against either of us, and then we could follow. Bishop Esher, however, insisted, that if either of us knew of any wrong he had been guilty of, either personal or official, that we should state wherein it consisted, and offered that as far as was in his power he would right such wrong. I at once responded in direct language that I had no grievance of any kind so far as Bishop Esher was concerned. That he had at all times treated me courteously and brotherly, and had been as considerate as a father in all things. Bishop Dubs' reply was: "I have nothing to say." I insisted, that if Dubs had anything in his heart against either of us, he should comply with the directions of our Discipline and the Word of God, and state what it is; that we could never adjust matters unless he would speak out manfully. Pleadings were, however, of no avail. Bishop Dubs neither consented to state his grievances, if he had any, nor would he say he had none, nor would he suggest any other method or plan, but simply reiterated, "I have nothing to say." Neither did he in any manner intimate that he was ready to right matters if he could be convinced that he had wronged any one. In fact, the only thing he consented to do was to listen to what we had to state concerning himself. Although Dubs' attitude and actions were such that an adjustment seemed improbable, and Bishop Esher being confirmed in his opinion that nothing would be accomplished, was about ready to give up the effort, I continued to insist that as Bishop Dubs had consented to hear what Bishop Esher had to say, he should proceed. So finally Bishop Esher agreed he would state his grievances, but said he would not mention such matters as were purely of a personal character, adding that he was willing to bury these without so much as mentioning them, but only such as related to Bishop Dubs' official actions. He then in detail pointed out 1, Bishop Dubs' attack upon him at the session of the Illinois Conference in Washington, Ill.; 2, His conduct in reference to the appointment of Bro. Hintze to Germany, in which he had grossly violated the truth as well as official confidence, and reflected upon Bishop Esher's integrity; 3, His letter to Dr. George. In all three of these points he charged Bishop Dubs with being guilty both of falsehood and slander. *Bishop Dubs listened attentively to the statements of Bishop Esher, and when the latter had finished, took his hat and left the room without in any way explaining or denying anything that had been said against him, in fact, without saying anything at all!*

Thus ended the second attempt at "arbitration." No thoughtful person will fail to see that such conduct on the part of Bishop Dubs could only make the matter worse, and was calculated to destroy every vestige of confidence in the purity of his motives. How much confidence could I hereafter place in any desire he might suggest to have peace and harmony? My conviction from this time forward was that Dubs meant war to the bitter end. If not, why pursue such a course, when matters were at issue involving the welfare of the Church? An honest, conscientious man would have defended his course if he believed himself right, and would gladly have corrected it if convinced of being wrong. Bishop Dubs was unwilling to do either. At that time no judicial finding had been had upon these matters, and if there had been any willingness on the part of Bishop Dubs to meet his colleagues with any reasonable proposition to right the wrongs of which he was guilty—guilty without any doubt whatever—things could have been adjusted. Why, if, as he has said in his defence, he could not entrust himself to Bishop Esher and myself, did he not suggest an attempt at adjustment in the presence of other parties? He would have found both of us more than willing. He at no time expressed or manifested the least desire to have the relations between himself and his colleagues adjusted, nor did he make any proposition looking to such a desirable end. The only exception was that about six months previous to the General Conference in Allentown, Pa., at a time he believed himself to be in a precarious condition of health, he referred to the matter in a private letter to Bishop Esher.

Up to this time although I knew Bishop Dubs was guilty of grave faults, to express it mildly, both in his personal and official conduct, still I had in a manner clung to him and had defended him as far as I could. We were on good terms at the time of our election in 1875. We were nearly of the same age. It was but natural we should be intimate, personally and officially. Bishop Esher is of a more retiring disposition, older, more sedate. Moreover upon several occasions we had been on opposite sides on ecclesiastical questions, so that while there was no personal feeling, there was no particular personal intimacy. But his stern sense of truth and righteousness, yet his mild, kind, and fatherly conduct, his repeated avowed willingness to right any wrong he might have done—as compared with the apparently politic course, the seeking after self-aggrandizement and personal popularity often at the expense of truth, and even at the expense of the reputation of his fellow laborers pursued by Bishop Dubs, and the latter's entire unwillingness even to make an effort to adjust difficulties, which were threatening the welfare and unity of the Church—had a tendency not only to build a middle wall of partition between the latter and myself, but also to greatly weaken my confidence in him; while upon the other hand I was drawn closer to Bishop Esher. I was convinced by this time that Dubs wanted war and not peace. Like his helper, Rev. H. B. Hartzler, he had "chosen the stormy voyage," and at that time seemed to be entirely confident of accomplishing his purpose, namely "to put Esher down" and he become THE Bishop of the Evangelical Association.

THE THIRD ATTEMPT AT ADJUSTMENT.

The misunderstandings between the Bishops had become so well known throughout the Church that when the General Conference met in Allentown, Pa., in 1883, a delegate to that body, Rev. Jesse Yeakel, called the attention of the General Conference to the situation. After spending some considerable time in discussing how to proceed, it was finally resolved that the conference should sit as a committee of the whole, and hear the Bishops. Rev. C. K. Fehr was elected chairman of the committee. Space will not permit us to enter into a description of all the details of the proceedings had. It will suffice to say that Bishop Esher, in his statements of the difficulties, plainly told the delegates to the General Conference, sitting in the capacity of a committee, *that he had lost all confidence in the integrity and veracity of Bishop Dubs*, and also plainly stated the reasons why, giving an account of most of the occurrences which have been described in these pages, except the rumors reflecting upon Bishop Dubs' social purity. Bishop Esher also read a letter Bishop Dubs had addressed to the writer which was so exceedingly ugly, that it took Dubs about a week to explain it. The writer also stated to the General Conference delegates very plainly that *the matter at issue involved the veracity of the Bishops of the Evangelical Association, and hence needed a thorough investigation*. By what right then can Bishops

EFFORTS TO ADJUST DIFFICULTIES. 71

Esher and Bowman be accused, as they have been by friend and foe, for allowing these accusations to run on so long without bringing them to the attention of the Church? Had we not told Bishop Dubs of his wrong-doing personally, orally and in writing, in accordance with the directions of our Discipline and the Word of God? Had we not repeated our accusations against him in the presence of the general officers of the Church in Cleveland, Ohio? Did we not make full and explicit statements of these things to the delegates of the General Conference in the city of Allentown, Pa., in 1883? What more ought we to have done? What more *could* we have done than to inform the Church of the facts? After stating the facts to the representatives of the Church in their official capacity as delegates to the General Conference, does not rather the responsibility for continuing a man in the episcopal office with such accusations against his character rest upon the Church itself? Instead of consenting to a compromise, where questions affecting the moral character of the highest officials of the Church were involved, the most searching investigation into the alleged charges ought to have been made and the guilty punished and the innocent exonerated.

After Bishop Esher's and Bishop Bowman's statements had been made, Bishop Dubs occupied days in endeavoring to defend himself and explain his course, first denying some things, then afterwards acknowledging them. Especially was this the case in regard to what he had said in Canada about the "Peace Meeting" in Chicago to several brethren, namely that "Bishop Esher was as deep in the mud as the others in the mire." At first he denied it, but when confronted with the evidence he admitted it. So also what he had said to Rev. R. Mott, whom he had offered an official position in the event of his working for Dubs. At first he denied it, but when Bro. Mott arose to confront him he hurriedly acknowledged it to be true. In endeavoring to defend himself he was forced into the necessity of falsely reading a postal card, *a la* John Schneider, written by

Rev. R. Yeakel, in which, however, he was immediately exposed. In order to strengthen his position he adroitly managed to give John Schneider an opportunity to empty his vials of wrath and slander upon Bishop Esher before the representatives of the Church. Finally after exhausting every resource, and bringing forward every conceivable imaginary point to excuse the course he had pursued, when it would have been Bishop Esher's time to present the evidence to sustain the accusations he had made against Dubs, *and as he was in the act of doing so*, Dubs very well knowing how damaging that evidence would be—knowing that all his sophistry could not explain it away—came before the General Conference and at least to some extent acknowledged his wrong-doing. However, this confession even was made in a manner peculiar to himself. Many of the delegates were wearied listening to the statements and counter statements which were made, were eager for peace at almost any price. Hence after Bishop Dubs' "confession" was made, a resolution was adopted requesting the Bishops to meet and if possible to make an amicable adjustment between themselves. For this purpose the Bishops met in the house of Bishop Bowman on the evening of October 18, 1883. The writer in describing what took place at that meeting will again use either his official title or the personal pronoun in order if possible not to be misunderstood.

Bishop Dubs had not stated any of his grievances against his colleagues before the delegates of the General Conference. He had acted wholly on the defensive, except in one instance when he attempted in an exceedingly dramatic manner, to reflect upon Bishop Bowman because he had allowed Bishop Esher to read the exceedingly ugly letter he had written him. He had said, however, he would tell us privately what he had against us, thereby intimating he actually had some grievance. Hence when we met Bishop Esher, after stating that he had no faith whatever in an amicable adjustment between ourselves, that the General Conference to which we were amenable ought to have adjusted matters in accordance with the provisions of our discipline—demanded that before we proceed Bishop Dubs must state what he had against either of us, as he had intimated he had something to tell us; Bishop Dubs refused at first to do so, whereupon Bishop Esher declared that any further attempts at adjustment were at an end, and that next morning he would tender his resignation as Bishop and end his official responsibility. Bishop Dubs, seeing that he could no longer evade the issue, then said: "I think you accuse me too severely about the lost letter." *This was all!* After all the efforts made by Bishop Esher on former occasions, and during the time occupied by the General Conference in looking into those things, and the almost desperate attempt when we had met to adjust matters, this was all that could be got out of him. Against me Dubs had not even a word to say. Yet he had left the General Conference under the impression that he had something serious against us both. Bishop Esher then stated another condition which he considered necessary to an adjustment, namely, that Bishop Dubs sever his close and intimate alliance with those persons in Illinois with whom the disturbance had its commencement. Up to this stage of the proceedings I had remained silent, then, however, I spoke to Bishop Dubs, kindly, but earnestly, saying: "Brother Dubs, if you will not sever your connection with those persons they will drag you into the pit." Our conversation was in German. The exact language I used was: *Sie stuerzen dich in den Abgrund.* Upon this remark Bishop Dubs arose, considerably excited, and said, "How can I tear myself loose from them? How can I? Here is this William Huelster, I believe every word contained in Bro. Wittenwyler's charges against him. He has not only defrauded Wittenwyler and others, but he has also defrauded John Schneider, and if he will not make matters right before the next session of the Illinois Conference, Schneider will bring charges against him. And here is this Stamm. Why must he sit in the highest body in our Church?" Thus Dubs spoke of his friends and helpers on that memorable evening. Finally after other things were discussed Bishop Dubs, having become apparently quite penitent, said: "*The greatest mistake of my life is that at the time of my election to the episcopal office, I resolved to put Bishop Esher down, and that I continued to act in this manner.*" Then turning to me he said, "And you Thomas helped me to this idea when you came and said, we must have you for Bishop in order to put Esher down." I replied indignantly that the first part of what he said, that I had been strongly in favor of his election as Bishop was true, but that the latter, that we needed him "to put Esher down" was unqualifiedly untrue. That I had said no such thing to him then nor at any other time, adding, "you know that Bishop Esher treated both of us not only in a brotherly, but even fatherly manner." This silenced Dubs entirely on this point. He very well knew that he was attempting to load some of his guilt upon another by a false accusation. Such a thought had never entered my mind. After a discussion of minor points Bishop Dubs said: "If you brethren cannot or will not take from me the charge of untruthfulness, I will be compelled to strap my bundle and go home." (*Meinen Buendel schnueren und nach Hause gehen*). He then pleaded for his wife and his children, that he was raising his boys for the Church, etc. Bishop Esher notwithstanding remained firm in his position, not in any manner to compromise the matter. Mrs. Dubs, a noble, pious, consecrated Christian woman, had called at my house on the morning of that day, and in a private interview with Mrs. Bowman, said that she had pleaded with her husband, the previous night until two o'clock in the morning, on her knees, with her Bible open before her, that she had prevailed, and that Mr. Dubs would come into the conference that morning and confess his wrong-doing, adding, as the tears streamed from her face, "I hope Bishops Esher and Bowman will then deal mercifully with him." Before I went into our front room on that eventful evening, my wife pleaded with me to remember Sister Dubs, and go as far as possible to adjust the difficulties peacefully.

Under these circumstances I allowed my sympathies to overrule my better judgment and suggested that probably we might go before the General Conference and say that at least the matter about the Dr. George letter may possibly rest upon misunderstanding, and joined Bishop Dubs in pleading with Bishop Esher to compromise the matter. Finally, although very reluctantly, Bishop Esher consented to adopt my suggestion, to say that the Dr. George letter matter may possibly rest upon a misunderstanding. Bishop Dubs of course being at once fully agreed to such an arrangement. All other accusations against Dubs of deliberate falsehood, etc., nine in number, remained as they had been presented to General Conference, without any modification whatever. And there they stand unchanged, and the evidence for all of them is at hand.

There was no other way left to save Bishop Dubs from ecclesiastical ruin and disgrace. Had the evidence been presented to the General Conference it could not have passed it by. It would have been compelled to convict him. *And the evidence was in our possession then as it is now.* Dubs had led us to hope that in the future, if we now save him and his family from disgrace, he would be a different man and pursue a different course. In our great desire for peace, and if possible to save his talents for the Church, we allowed ourselves to be again deceived by his hypocrisy. And now the man whom to save from ecclesiastical ruin and disgrace we stooped to a questionable compromise is conscienceless enough even to deny what he admitted on that occasion, and to ridicule us for what we did solely to save him and his family from disgrace, injury and ruin. Can deeper depths of iniquity be imagined?

The next morning Bishop Esher stated to the General Conference what had been done, and went so far as to relieve Bishop Dubs from the accusation of falsehood in the Dr. George letter matter, accepting the adjustment in good faith, notwithstanding his reluctance to enter into it and his fear of another deception and betrayal. Alas, his fear was only too well founded. Before twenty-four hours had passed by, both of us were convinced that we had been deceived; that, being out of his dilemma, he would continue in the same course he had hitherto pursued, and continue his sinister relations with the unscrupulous ring in the Illinois Conference as before. Notwithstanding his assertions in our meeting about the corruption and dishonesty of William Huelster the two were seen walking arm in arm within twenty-four hours after that memorable evening.

The political scheming of "Dubs' minority party" probably reached its acme at that General Conference. Although in the "minority," yet by political scheming they succeeded in re-electing Rev. H. B. Hartzler as Editor of the *Evangelical Messenger*, in defeating Rev. H. J. Bowman, as Editor of the *Living Epistle* and English Sunday-School Literature, and electing Rev. P. W. Raidabaugh in his stead. They succeeded even in electing Rev. S. L. Wiest to a General Conference office, although by his conduct, as Corresponding Secretary of the Missionary Society, he had made himself very obnoxious to the Church. In the election of bishops the meanest and most dishonest electioneering tactics were adopted by Dubs' party. Among those who had fully entered into their plans it was fully understood that no one would vote for the re-election either of Esher or Bowman, and neither did they. Among those who had not taken sides, at least not in a pronounced manner, Dubs' political workers said: "Now, that the difficulties between the Bishops have been adjusted, we must re-elect all three; however, Esher and Bowman will be re-elected at any rate, and it would not be good policy to have their majority over Dubs so large, therefore you ought to vote solid for Dubs. Among the pronounced friends of Esher and Bowman they said: "Now, as the difficulties between the Bishops are adjusted, let us all vote as one man for the re-election of all of them." In this wise they succeeded in depriving Esher and Bowman of votes they would otherwise have received, induced delegates to vote for Dubs who had not intended to do so, and succeeded in reducing the vote for the first two, and increasing that of Dubs. After the election was over they congratulated their Bishop and themselves upon the success of their scheme.

Notwithstanding all these efforts to adjust matters so that there would be peace, the reader will find that the war still went on. R. Dubs considered it unsafe from this time forward to appear "as the principal party therein," hence he kept himself more in the background, and allowed his lieutenants publicly at least to assume the leadership, although in every assault made on his colleagues, and on the various Boards of the Church, and other general officials, he was in full accord and sympathy with the "minority," and no doubt consulted with them in all their plans.

Upon his return to Cleveland, O., from his episcopal visits he was frequently closeted with Rev. H. B. Hartzler, the editor of the *Messenger*, for hours before going to his own home, though he had been absent from home for weeks. He had no such important business with any other church officer except S. L. Wiest, Clewell etc. Meanwhile Hartzler was slashing away right and left, at every body who did not join "the party."

At that time the "minority" did not want peace. They considered agitation the proper thing for their interests. Hence Rev. H. B. Hartzler chose the "stormy voyage," while he himself acknowledged he might have had quiet sailing, had he so chosen. The "war cry" of the "minority" was "Bishop Esher must be put down." Not that they hated him more than others whom they could not control and use for their purposes, but because they considered him the one man in their way towards becoming the majority. So they were determined not to cease their labors until this end was accomplished.

There was still another reason why these efforts at arbitration failed. Moral wrong had been done. Truth and Right had been trampled into the dust. God's law had been transgressed.

Rudolph Dubs and many of his followers had made themselves guilty of falsehood, deception and other sins. Sin cannot be condoned. It must be repented of, put away, and pardon sought and found. The recent proposition to "arbitrate" involved all these matters. It was not entertained, and could not have been entertained by the Church, because there were allegations of "immorality" made and even judicially acted upon. These allegations were either true or they were untrue. The proposition to compromise with immorality was simply absurd, to say nothing of insurmountable legal hindrances in the way. The Evangelical Association would have forfeited her sovereignty and endangered her existence if she had set aside her own laws and authority and allowed unauthorized persons to adjust her internal affairs. It was an impossibility. Think of the position of the parties who held the so-called trials at Chicago and Reading! They declare their victims guilty of "immorality," then for this crime of which they declare they found them guilty, "clearly convicted," they proceed to "suspend" them from all their official functions. This fact is published to the world in almost every secular paper in this country, and to some extent in other countries of the world. A few months afterwards the principal parties engaged in this work declare their willingness, yea eagerness, to submit the "immorality" of which they declared their victims guilty.—"clearly convicted"—to arbitration! Could stronger proof of their insincerity be given? Sincerity, and a sense of Truth and Righteousness have not figured in the schemes of the seceders. Success, success by any means, was the goal of their ambition. Some one who was well acquainted with the spirit of the rebellion, and who knows its entire history said of it as early as 1887: "This rebellion was conceived in iniquity, born in depravity, raised in corruption, and has contaminated every man prominently connected with it." The history of this revolt has fully justified the description given above. Furthermore its history has proven that nothing but the strong arm of ecclesiastical law backed by the much stronger arm of civil law is mighty enough to subdue its rebellious spirit. It has even defied and evaded the arm of civil law, and cries out against the courts of the land as against the courts of the Church. Such is the usual course of iniquity.

CHAPTER VI.

The difficulties connected with our Mission in Japan.

The heathen mission of our Church was established by the General Conference at its session in Philadelphia, Pa., in 1875. The lamented Dr. Krecker and Rev. A. Halmhuber were the first missionaries. Afterwards Prof. W. E. Walz was also appointed. In 1880, Rev. Jacob Hartzler was chosen by the Executive Committee as Superintendent of our mission work in Japan. The choice of Bro. Hartzler was very peculiar. The majority of the Committee consented to his appointment with much doubt and many misgivings. His age, his ability to accomplish very little while seeming to be very busy, and his lack of executive ability, were very much against him in the sober judgment of the majority of the Committee. The Committee had been searching for some one to go to Japan to take charge of our mission work but had not succeeded, and was exceedingly anxious to find some one to go. At this meeting Bishop Dubs presented the name of Rev. J. Hartzler for this position, presenting the proposition in an extraordinary, dramatic manner, intimating that it was a special revelation from God and a direction of Providence, so that the sober judgment of the brethren might be overcome by sentiment, and the appointment was made. Afterwards it was discovered that the thing had been regularly planned and this style and method adopted in order to close our eyes against the intrigue.

After Mr. Hartzler had been in Japan several years difficulties arose, so that the Board of Missions at its session in Lindsay, O., found it necessary to pass a vote of dissatisfaction with Hartzler's administration. The dissatisfaction in Japan seemed to increase from year to year, and the confidence at home in his management seemed to decrease in about the same proportion. Subsequently Rev. W. F. Voegelein was sent as missionary to Japan. Bishop Dubs was very eager for Br. Voegelein's appointment, claiming that he and Bro. Hartzler were very good friends, and that his appointment would be welcome news to the Superintendent who also disired Bro. V.'s appointment. However, nothwithstanding this intimate friendship Bro. Voegelein, very soon after his arrival in Japan, discovered that the management was very deficient. Finally Prof. Walz ventured to call attention of the Superintendent to what he (Walz) considered inexpedient in the management, and also to the deplorable condition of the work on the mission in general. The Superintendent then requested Prof. Walz to put his complaints in writing, which he did, and handed the paper to him. *For venturing this criticism upon the Superintendent's management, he formulated charges against Prof. Walz* and forwarded them to the Executive Committee of Cleveland, Ohio. Upon receiving these charges the Committee was called together by the Chairman, and upon due consideration referred the charges to the Bishops, upon the ground that the Committee as such had no legal right to try charges against a minister. The Committee also expressed the opinion that one of the Bishops should visit Japan and examine into affairs generally. This action was ratified and concurred in by the Board of Missions at its session in Cleveland, Ohio, in October 1884. The Board of Bishops at a subsequent meeting appointed the senior Bishop J. J. Esher to undertake the arduous journey and the responsible and unpleasant labor. It is somewhat suggestive that there was some opposition from certain quarters, mostly from persons professing especial friendship for Rev. J. Hartzler, against the action of the Board in requesting a Bishop to visit Japan in order to investigate the condition of our mission work, which cost the Church thousands of dollars annually. Especially did it seem somewhat remarkable in view of the fact that the

Superintendent had preferred charges against one of his subordinates, which certainly could be investigated in Japan only, in the presence of the accuser and the accused—more especially in view of the fact that the reports from the mission field were so very conflicting. The Superintendent had been sending glowing reports of the condition of the mission both to the Board and to the *Evangelical Messenger*. His brother, Rev. H. B. Hartzler, then editor of the *Messenger*, always corroborated these reports, and in strong language eulogized the condition of things in Japan. He even informed the Church through the *Messenger*, that his brother, after being in Japan but a short time, comparatively speaking, was able to preach in the Japanese language, a representation which was afterwards discovered to have been wholly untrue. Upon the other hand the reports sent from the other missionaries represented the mission as being in a deplorable condition. Were these special friends of the Superintendent concious of the real condition of things and afraid of the truth? It is suggestive also that this opposition against an investigation of the facts came from the very element which afterwards seceded from the Church. As heretofore stated they at no time wanted an investigation into the facts of anything connected with our difficulties. Was it because they were aware the facts were against them?

A few extracts from the evidence of the missionaries in regard to the real condition of the mission immediately prior to Bishop Esher's visit to Japan at that time may here be in place. In a letter dated July 31, 1884, Bro. Voegelein wrote: "After I had been here three months, I attended a kind of quarterly conference, at which time the native preachers seriously complained about unworthy members, and the statement was made that hardly one in five attended our services. When I asked the reason of this, the answer was given that many had long since gone back. We baptize too soon, other churches talk about it. *We have three appointments (preaching places) for us three missionaries, six women, and five native preachers.*"

Prof. Walz said to the Superintendent: "I do not see how you could succeed in making things worse without undisguisedly showing a complete disregard of what ought to be more dear and sacred to your heart than aught else—the peace and success of the mission."

Prof. Walz in his report of the mission at Odowarocho says: "A close investigation brought, among others, the following facts to light: One of our members was in prison, another was a defrauder and a fugitive from justice, another had left his own wife and had gone with another woman, another lived in open adultery, another had committed theft; one woman had openly returned to idolatry, and others were under suspicion of paying homage to idols." *All these were kept on the records and reported by Rev. J. Hartzler to the Board as members.*

After Bishop Esher had appointed Bro. Voegelein to Mitoshirocho the latter reported as follows: "The Superintendent gave me names of 59 adult members, but of these only from eight to ten attended our services, *and so it had been for a year or two*. Some of those reported as members in the last report of the Superintendent had long since disappeared, but were all included in his report to America, and the Church in America rejoiced over this report. About 12 or 14 instead of 59 were actually there."

The same deplorable facts were true of Hinoyeki. Here Rev. J. Hartzler had baptized 80 persons in a few weeks, and he and his brother H. B. Hartzler made a great ado about it in the *Messenger;* in a very short time afterwards only about ten of the whole number attended our services. The Superintendent afterwards reported 42 members, when in reality we did not have more than ten. The facts were these. While the Superintendent reported officially that we had 205 members in Japan, we actually, at the most liberal estimate, did not have over 50, and not more than 30 attending our services! *We had four appointments and twenty seven paid persons employed in our work!* Neither Bro. Voegelein nor Prof. Walz had received any appointment from the Superintendent. There was so much dissatisfaction with the Superintendent, Rev. J. Hartzler, among the Japanese membership, that they had decided to send a petition to the home authorities for his removal from the field. These things may suffice to give the reader a proper insight into the condition of the mission at the time of Bishop Esher's visit. And yet the Superintendent continued to deceive the Church by his untruthful reports, in which he was materially aided by his brother, then editor of the *Messenger*; evidence for all of which is at hand.

In this connection the Romanization farce, which Rev. Jacob Hartzler and his brother Rev. H. B. Hartzler and others attempted to impose upon the Church, and with which for a while they actually succeeded in deceiving a great many, must also be mentioned. According to their representations it was made to appear that the language of Japan was being really revolutionized in a very short period of time, and that henceforth no further necessity existed for missionaries from Christian lands to study the language, but by means of this new method they could at once enter upon the work of Gospel preaching. It was a gross deception imposed upon the Church.

In 1882 Rev. Jacob Hartzler reported in the *Evangelical Messenger*: "*I can now preach in the Japanese language.*" On the 24th of October 1882, Rev. H. B. Hartzler said in his editorial notes in the *Messenger*: "The Superintendent of our Japan mission is to be congratulated that he has already suceeded in mastering the Japanese language, to such an extent as to enable him to preach the Gospel in that difficult tongue." In these statements, by these two brothers, there was not a vestige of truth. Possibly the editor did not know better, although a man of his pretensions ought to have known better. Jacob Hartzler, however, knew he was deceiving the Church on this language question just as well as he knew he had deceived the Church in his official reports in reference to the condition of the mission. When Bishop Esher came to Japan in 1885 the

Superintendent could not even introduce the Bishop to the congregation he was to address, but was compelled to employ the service of an interpreter, and yet *two and a half years previous* he had informed the Church: "I now preach in the Japanese language," and his brother, the editor, congratulated him upon "mastering the Japanese language!" That the Church re-called the one and deposed the other of these two brothers has to this day been heralded to the world as an excuse for rebellion, and a sufficient cause for making all the disturbance since the General Conference of 1887!

Upon Bishop Esher's arrival in Japan it did not take him very long to discover that the representations made by Prof. Walz and Bro. Voegelein were correct, and that the mission was indeed in "a deplorable condition." The investigation at which he was compelled to preside in view of the charges preferred by Rev. J. Hartzler against Prof. W. E. Walz, called forth all the facts and circumstances connected with the mission, besides what he was compelled to see and hear. The charges were that Prof. Walz in his criticism of Hartzler's administration had assailed his moral and official character. These charges were fully set forth in twenty different specifications. Prof. Walz's defence was that the assertions he had made in reference to Hartzler's management were true and hence he was not guilty. It took twelve days to submit the evidence. Every question put to the witnesses, with the answer, together with every ruling of the chair was taken down in writing. During this trial Prof Walz reiterated, even in much stronger language, what he had previously stated in reference to Jacob Hartzler, namely, that he was *utterly incompetent, insincere, dishonest, and untruthful*. The entire record of the trial is in our possession and can be produced whenever necessary. So also the speeches both of the accuser and accused are in our possession.

After Bishop Esher had returned from Japan he selected a Committee to decide the case composed of the following persons: R. Dubs, Thomas Bowman, M. Lauer, R. Yeakel, Wm.

Yost, Wm. Horn, C. A. Thomas, S. Heininger, and S. L. Wiest. These were precisely the same persons to whom Rev. J. Hartzler had originally sent his charges against Prof. Walz, hence he at least could find no fault with the Bishop's selection. Now, however, they did not sit as the Executive Committee, but as individual ministers of the Church. This Committee read the entire record as it had been taken down in Japan, as well as the speeches of the accused and accuser, and after weighing carefully all the facts presented reported that Prof. Walz was *not guilty* of the charges brought against him by the Superintendent. Of the nine ministers, who sat as the trial committee, all voted for this report except S. L. Wiest, and even *he* could not vote against it, but desired to remain neutral. Even Bishop Dubs, who in the official papers of the Church had claimed to be an especial friend of Jacob Hartzler, voted with the rest that Walz was not guilty. The accusations which Prof. Walz had made against Rev. Jacob Hartzler were incompetency, insincerity, dishonesty, and untruthfulness. For saying these things the charges against him had been brought by Hartzler. In the course of the trial Walz had boldly repeated his assertions, and produced such facts in his defence, that the Committee, including Rudolph Dubs, was compelled to declare the person, who had made such grave charges against Jocob Hartzler—accusations which Hartzler alleged assailed his moral and official character—as NOT GUILTY. Hence in the opinion of this Committee Walz's accusations against Jacob Hartzler were founded on fact, and were therefore true. Prof. Walz's charges against Hartzler of utter incompetency, insincerity, dishonesty, and untruthfulness were proven by the evidence. THUS STANDS THE RECORD. Prof. Walz had charged Jacob Hartzler with being the chief cause why the mission was in such a deplorable condition. The facts presented by him in his defence prove the truthfulness of his accusations, and he is adjudged *not guilty.* Prof. Walz's accusations, says the Committee, including his special and intimate friend R. Dubs, stand vindicated by the facts!

And when this man, who had deceived the Church by false official reports, by falsely reporting himself as able to preach in the Japanese language, and who had virtually been found guilty of incompetency, of insincerity, of dishonesty, and untruthfulness, and is finally recalled, though after a long and patient waiting on the part of the Church for improvement, a faction in the Church seizes upon it as a pretext for causing the great and wicked disturbance inaugurated in 1886 and 1887 and continued to this date!

The annual meeting of the Board of Missions, after Bishop Esher's return from Japan, was held in Indianapolis, Ind., in October 1885. As the Board of Missions had referred the charges against one of the missionaries in Japan, brought by the Superintendent, to the Board of Bishops for investigation, and in addition had requested one of the Bishops to visit Japan to inquire into the condition of the work, it was expected that the Bishop who had been sent, would furnish the Board with an exhaustive report. Rev. H. B. Hartzler, although not a member of the Board, also appeared on the scene. Why he came was soon discovered, namely, to circulate secretly, among such members of the Board, as he knew to be in sympathy and harmony with the laudable (?) effort "to put Esher down," a circular intended to reflect upon the official report, which he knew would be made, and also to prejudice the members against its correctness. What other purpose could there have been? And if what this circular alleged was true, why circulate it secretly and only among a certain class? And why was the brother through whom it was discovered made the subject of so much personal abuse? Truth need not adopt such means. While the Bishop was thousands of miles away, the editor assailed him publicly, but when compelled to meet him on equal terms, then he hides himself in darkness, and does it secretly. However the hidden work of darkness came to light. One of the persons, who since played such a conspicuous part in the rebellion against the Evangelical Association and of course received a copy of the Editor's secret circular, let it lie in his sleeping apartment, where it was found and the plot exposed. The Board passed a resolution denouncing in strong terms such a disreputable course. One of the specifications of the charges which were subsequently brought against the editor at the General Conference of 1887 recited what has been stated above. It reads as follows : "In this that within three years last past the said H. B. Hartzler, secretly and in a manner wholly abhorrent to an honest man, unworthy of a professed Christian and reprehensible in a minister of the Gospel, did publish and distribute so-called pamphlets or printed circulars for the purpose of influencing and prejudicing the minds of certain members of the General Board of Missions against the truth." This specification was sustained by the findings of the General Conference. It was the first time in the history of our Church that an attempt of this kind was made. The Board felt it had been insulted and outraged by one of the general officers of the Church whose duty it would have been to defend the Board as far as truth would permit. After H. B. Hartzler had thus disturbed the otherwise peaceful session of the Board he went back to his editorial sanctum and informed the Church how stormy the sessions of its Board of Missions had been ! And on account of this man, and his brother Jacob, the rebellion was inaugurated at Buffalo, N. Y., in 1887 by R. Dubs and his followers !

At that meeting of the Board of Missions, Bishop Esher made a full report of the condition of things as he discovered them to be, giving the mission and the Superintendent the full benefit of every doubtful question, as the developments of the future abundantly prove. The deplorable facts were stated as mildly as possible, in the opinion of some much too mildly, as the Bishop was compelled subsequently in the unfortunate controversy forced upon him by H. B. Hartzler, to state a good many things as they ought probably to have been stated in the beginning. Consideration for Jacob Hartzler and his friends had prompted the Bishop to be as mild as he was. The Superintendent had informed the Church two years previous that he could preach in the Japanese language, for which he was congratulated by his brother the editor. Certainly when Bishop Esher discovered this shameful deception he might have used very strong language. Most men would have done so. Instead the Bishop in his report uses the following language: "Of the present missionaries none are able to pray or conduct worship or official transactions, or transact any other business official or otherwise with the natives. All these things must be done by all through interpreters. Only the sisters Krecker and Hudson are partially able to pray in Japanese, and with readiness to impart religious instruction, and converse with the natives." Of the Romanization swindle he used the following mild terms: "It is at best a very imperfect and defective makeshift for any one who does not know the language and does not really understand what he reads."

Besides the report on the condition of affairs in our heathen mission, Bishop Esher also made some suggestions in reference to methods for carrying on the work in the future, among others the necessity of a course of instruction previous to baptism. The Superintendent's usage had been to baptize almost any one who applied practically indiscriminately, upon a mere profession, and by this method had brought disgrace upon the cause, and came well nigh ruining the mission. Bishop Esher's original idea had been a course of six months instruction, but he modified his opinion in some measure to please the Superintendent, because of the latter's opposition to any time being devoted to instruction previous to baptism. Hence upon his return he suggested a course of four months instruction to precede baptism. This suggestion was made to the Executive Committee, in session at Cleveland, O. But upon motion of Bishop Dubs, the time was changed to six months. This being in accord with Bishop Esher's original idea, he suggested to the Board of Missions, that a course of six months instruction should precede baptism. This suggestion was unanimously adopted by the Board. How Bishop Esher and the Board of Missions were afterwards assailed by the Editor of the *Messenger*, and Rev. D. B. Byers, in a long series of articles, is a matter of history. And how Bishop R. Dubs, who was the author of the resolution of the Board for the six months course of instruction stood by in silence and allowed his colleague to be maltreated by his especial friends is also a fact of history. Furthermore how the editor assailed and allowed others to assail in the official paper the official action of the Church through her Board of Missions, but refused to allow the official actions of the Church to be defended in her official organ is also a matter of history.

The Board of Missions accepted the Bishop's report. It was spread upon the minutes and ordered to be published in our weeklies, the *Botschafter* and *Messenger*. The Board also adopted the Bishop's suggestions, especially that referring to the necessity of acquiring a knowledge of the Japanese language. The Board furthermore declared that the failure on the part of any missionary to comply with this requirement, should be regarded a sufficient reason to be recalled. The office of Superintendent, the one-man power arrangement, was abolished, and in its stead, "A Managing Committee" was appointed.

No sooner had the Board adjourned, and the editor, who had gone to Indianapolis to carry on his warfare against the Bishop, returned home, than he wrote a very ugly, and in many respects untruthful editorial against the Board and its actions, fiercely assailing the official proceedings of a representative body of the Church in its official organ.

Later on, when the first half of the Bishop's report was published in the *Messenger*, the editor also assailed its correctness, and called upon his correspondents who might be so inclined, to attack it, announcing at the same time his intention to do his share in carrying on the war against it. In order, if possible, to avoid public controversy and needless agitation throughout the Church, a meeting of the Executive Committee was called, at which all the members were present, including Bishop Dubs. At this meeting the Committee adopted the following resolutions, preceded, however, by a lengthy preamble, setting forth what Rev. H. B. Hartzler had said in his editorial, concerning the business of the Board of Missions, mildly reminding him that his statements were incorrect, and also of what he had said concerning Bishop Esher's report, and calling into question the right of an official editor thus to attack official reports and official actions in the official papers, thereby injuring our missionary interests:

"*Resolved*, That we hereby protest against this useless and injurious agitation, and most earnestly advise the Editor of the *Messenger*, to change his course in this respect."

This report *was adopted unanimously*. It was drawn up by a sub-committee, composed of Bishop Dubs, Rev. M. Lauer, and the writer. This advice was given to Rev. H. B. Hartzler, by men of large experience, including the three Bishops of the Church. It should have carried some weight. In view of his solemn ordination vows in which he obligated himself to reverence and obey his superiors in office, to follow even with a glad heart and willing mind their godly admonitions, as they may deem them expedient, he ought certainly to have at least respected the advice. *Upon the contrary it was received with sneers and treated with contempt.* His reply to this earnest and well meant advice at once revealed the flippant, erratic character of the man, with whom the Church was dealing. That answer alone and his conduct in connection therewith, aside from all his other sins, and the injury and ruin he wrought, should have been sufficient to depose him from the ministry and expel him from the Church, as it was a clear violation of his sacred ordination vows. And yet on account of this man, with whom the Church, notwithstanding the serious charges of which he was found guilty, dealt be leniently and mildly; and on account of his brother Jacob, who proved himself so wholly incompetent, unreliable, and treacherous, the great distraction in and following the General Conference of 1887 was commenced and carried on to this day!

Probably it might be well at this point to remind the reader of a few facts correlative to these difficulties. Invariably the element which finally held the rump conference in Philadelphia have been the assailants. In the first instance John Schneider, Wm. Huelster, and H. Rohland, under the editorship of Jacob Hartzler, were allowed the use of the *Messenger* publicly to attack the official actions of Bishop Esher. Next Bishop Dubs publicly assailed his senior colleague in the session of the Illinois Conference, at Washington, Ill. Then he assailed the proceedings of the Board of Bishops, and both of his colleagues personally, in a very reprehensible and cowardly manner, in his letter to Dr. A. C. George, doing it officially as Bishop of the Evangelical Association. Next, in order to explain his inconsistent actions, he publicly assailed the writer at a time when he knew the latter was physically in an entirely helpless condition. Next H. B. Hartzler assailed Bishop Esher's correspondence, while the latter was thousands of miles away from home attending to his official duties. Hereupon followed Hartzler's attack upon the Board of Missions, then upon Bishop Esher's report, as well as on the Bishop personally. Then in quick succession on the Executive Committee of the Board, on Rev. W. Horn, Editor of the *Botschafter*, for defending the Church against these attacks. This latter attack was a most unbrotherly assault. Then he attacked the Publishers, because they did not conform in their ideas of conducting their businsss to those of H. B. Hartzler. Of course, behind H. B. Hartzler stood the faction which afterwards rebelled against, and then seceded from the Church. He was but the mouthpiece of disloyalty.

Bishop Dubs at no time publicly questioned the correctness of Bishop Esher's report relative to the condition of our mission work in Japan. He evidently knew its statements were correct, and could not be successfully controverted. He knew how thorough Bishop Esher was in everything he did, and how exceedingly careful in making up his statements. Moreover he consented to all the suggestions made in reference to carrying on the work in the future, especially in regard to the Romanization theory. In fact, all of Bishop Esher's suggestions were adopted by the entire Board with more than usual unanimity. But this was not all. Bishop Dubs was also convinced of Rev. J. Hartzler's incompetency for the position he was occupying. To the writer he said previous to the meeting of the Board in Indianapolis, "Jacob Hartzler does not grasp the situation in Japan," and during the meeting of the Board he expressed himself unqualifiedly to both of his colleagues in favor of re-calling him, as he evidently was incompetent, but pleaded, that it would not be expedient to do so at once. "Only wait a year longer," was his plea, moreover he added, "after Jacob Hartzler reads our action in regard to Romanization, and the study of the language, he will undoubtedly return of his own accord." Bishop Esher, however, was confirmed in his conviction, that Hartzler should be re-called at once. Dubs continued his pleadings saying, "It won't do to be too severe at this time," so the writer suggested that probably after all it might be expedient and cause less agitation and less ill-will with his friends if we were to give him another year's trial; so finally Bishop Esher consented for the sake of peace that he would not personally urge his recall if the the Board would pass it by. For peace's sake Jacob Hartzler was allowed to remain and draw his salary another year.* Future develop-

---

* At the session of the East Pa. Conference, held in Norristown, Pa., in the Spring of 1888, after J. Hartzler's return from Japan, Bishop Dubs said to Rev. S. C. Breyfogel, in speaking of the situation in Japan, and of Rev. J. Hartzler, that there were two methods of operation in Japan, one the German, and the other the American method. The German, he said, insisted upon catechetical instruction, and a certain probationary time before administering baptism. The American, upon the other hand, he said, does not insist upon this, but baptizes on a profession of faith. In the course of his remarks Dubs emphatically declared that

ments made it evident that the conduct of Bishop Dubs was simply a ruse to gain time for "his friend Hartzler," hoping the opposition to his remaining in Japan would cease, and the Dubs party would still have a representative there to carry on its political work. It also became evident later that the attitude assumed by Bishop Dubs was well understood by "his friends" to have been assumed merely to serve them so much more effectually in their common cause. In the Central Pa. Conference Jacob Hartzler could be of no especial service to his party, but he could be in Japan, hence the course Dubs pursued. In fact it seems every movement the man made, every plan he adopted, everything he did, had the same end in view, namely, to gain supremacy in our Church for the party of which he was the head.

From the Fall of 1885, when Editor Hartzler commenced his attacks upon the actions of our official Boards, the *Evangelical*

---

he favored the so-called German method, and expressed his agreement with the views advanced and suggested by Bishop Esher after his return from Japan. Dubs furthermore stated to Bro. Breyfogel that he did not approve of all of the Hartzler methods, and gave it as his opinion that things would go better in Japan in the future, stating further that under the circumstances J. Hartzler's return was a necessity, but that he was not in accord with the way in which it was done.

A few days after the above statements had been made by Dubs, and after Jacob Hartzler made his address on Sunday evening, on which occasion he was chaperoned by Dubs, the obvious purpose of which was to awaken sympathy for Hartzler and opposition to the Board of Missions, Dubs in a private circle denounced the Board of Missions in unmeasured terms, characterizing the recalling of Hartzler after the expenditure of about $100,000 in Japan as a sin and a shame! Dubs also dilated on the success of Jacob Hartzler in Japan, and the great loss which the mission was now made to sustain by his recall. Bro. Breyfogel at once called Dubs' attention to the statements he had made to him privately only a few evenings previous, which were exactly the reverse of what he said now. As is the custom of Rudolph Dubs when confronted with his falsehoods, and his hypocrisy and misdeeds, by some one he knows can stand his ground, he abruptly dropped the matter and had no more to say.

Messenger ceased to be the organ of the Church, but was to all intents and purposes converted into the personal organ of Bishop Dubs, H. B. and Jacob Hartzler, and run in the especial interests of their party. Rev. D. B. Byers was invited to write a series of articles in defense of the opinion of the Hartzlers on the question of baptism in Japan, and diametrically opposed to the opinion of the Church as expressed by the Board of Missions, in which the entire Church had been represented, Byers even going so far as to assert that the Board of Missions had violated the fundamental laws of our Church, and of having trampled on the Word of God, in all of which he was endorsed by the editor, and even by Bishop Dubs, although he *seemed* to believe differently. Strange to say, the General Conference of 1887 adopted the views of the Board of Missions, nearly unanimously, and without debate, although these valiant assailants of the Board were present. Here they would have been met on equal ground, hence their courage failed them. The editor allowed anyone to assail the Board and Bishop Esher's report, but closed it against the Bishop in defense of his report and the action of the Board. No editor in the history of our Church ever presumed to arrogate to himself such an exercise of power as did H. B. Hartzler. In him tyranny and despotism seemed to have been personified. The *Evangelical Messenger* was the property of the Church, and was published at the expense of the Church, but had been converted into a personal organ to carry on war against the Church, and for two long years the Church endured this condition of things. Is it a wonder that the disaffection is larger in the English portion of our Church than in the German? For a quarter of a century the *Evangelical Messenger*, with only a short intermission, was in the hands of T. G. Clewell and the Hartzlers, each and all of them disloyal to the genius and polity of our Church. During the last two years of H. B. Hartzler's term the mask was entirely thrown off. What formerly had been done in an indirect and underhanded manner was now done openly and above board. The seeds of dissension were sown from a full hand and scattered broadcast throughout the Church And because the General Conference of 1887 said this business must stop in our official papers, a separate paper was established, in which disloyalty and rebellion should have free scope. Secession was the natural fruit to grow upon such a poisonous tree.

Perhaps in no other Church was there ever such a spectacle witnessed as the one which has here been briefly portrayed. The actions of the official Boards of the Church assailed — fiercely assailed, and misrepresented by the official editor and invited correspondents in the official organ of the Church, and closed against those who would defend the Church! At that time it did not seem necessary to hear " both sides." It was sufficient if the readers of the *Messenger* only heard the one side which had arrayed itself against the Church. Such a high-handed and arrogant course had never been even approached by any other of our editors in the history of our Church as did Henry B. Hartzler. Such "a centralization of power" was never before assumed by anyone, and it was not believed to exist. Yet these parties claim to be the very apostles of liberty and tolerance!

CHAPTER VII.

The General Conference of 1887, and what soon followed.

When the General Conference met in Buffalo, in 1887, as was no doubt fully expected by everyone in the Church who had read our Church papers during the preceding years, charges were preferred against Rev. H. B. Hartzler, editor of the *Evangelical Messenger*. The charge was: " Unchristian conduct, official misconduct, and grievous official offense as minister and as editor in our Church." The charge was minutely specified in seven general and nine sub-specifications.

After the charges and specifications were read, the accused raised an objection against the jurisdiction and legal right of the General Conference to try the case, contending that the charges should have been brought in a lower court. This objection was made in the face of the fact that the Board of Publication at its session immediately prior to the General Conference had referred the investigation of the official conduct of the officers amenable to it in the interim of General Conference, to the latter body. Bishop Esher being in the chair when this objection was made overruled it and decided that the General Conference had jurisdiction, and was the proper legal body to try the case. *The accused took no appeal from this decision.* The next day, Bishop Dubs being in the chair, the accused raised an objection against the form and manner of the specifications, contending that they were not in legal form, nor sufficiently specific, and appealed to the chair for a decision on this point, without any argument, that is without pointing out to the chair or the General Conference the alleged legal defects or wherein the specifications failed to specify. Bishop Dubs, *notwithstanding this fact that the accused did not point out the alleged defects in the specifications, was nevertheless quite ready with an elaborate and lengthy written opinion or ruling, really an argument in support of the position taken by the defense and ruled the charges out of the General Conference.* Can anyone in view of this fact doubt Dubs' relation to and connivance with this agitator and disturber of the peace of our Church? It had been freely predicted previous to the General Conference in Buffalo, N. Y., that no charges against Hartzler would be tried by that body. Was this the plan by which to prevent it? If the ruling of Bishop Dubs had been sustained, and the accusers had even brought their specifications in a different form, which is very questionable, the accused would no doubt have pleaded, as he did on a former occasion, that he did not have sufficient time for preparation for this new form, and thus have quashed the entire matter. But why interpose such technicalities against an investigation of the facts? Hartzler had all along boldly stated that the evidence for all his assertions, and even for his base insinuations, was in his possession. Certainly when an official editor in the official paper assails his own Church authorities, as he had done, he ought to have in his possession the indisputable facts wherewith to prove his accusations, and to court and even demand an investigation, not to try to evade it. It is a serious matter to make sweeping charges against the highest officials of a Church, and against the official Boards of a Church, thereby awakening distrust and causing disharmony, and, when it is done without cause, it is a crime. Or was the purpose of Bishop Dubs and Editor Hartzler in their combined effort to evade a trial at Buffalo a part of the program "to put Esher down"? H. B. Hartzler, Jacob Hartzler, D. B. Byers, and others of that party had again and again made the most serious accusations against Bishop Esher in the official Church papers; why did they not formulate charges against him at Buffalo? They had made them in the official organ of the Church and then closed that organ against an answer in defense. Why not—if they were so brave and so conscientious as they have all along claimed to be — meet the Bishop with their accusations at the proper time and place? In fact they were always exceedingly careful not to meet the Bishop with any accusations face to face where he would be upon equal terms with his accusers. H. B. Hartzler could write and print and secretly circulate a pamphlet seriously reflecting upon Bishop Esher's official work and character. He could do so in the paper of which he was editor and then refuse him a defense. But neither he nor any of his co-partners in the wicked crusade in which they had engaged had the manliness ever to meet him face to face with their accusations. Rev. E. L. Kiplinger indeed had summoned sufficient courage to notify Bishop Esher that he would prefer charges against him, but when the time came to do so, he backed down most ingloriously.

Had the plan of Rudolph Dubs and H. B. Hartzler and their associates succeeded at Buffalo to evade an investigation, of course Bishop Esher could not honorably have accepted a re-election, and so he would have been gotten out of the way. Here also history repeats itself. They wanted no investigation, but a resignation.

But to return to the scenes in the General Conference at Buffalo. An appeal was taken from Bishop Dubs' partisan and undisciplinary ruling, and the appeal was sustained by the General Conference, after which the trial proceeded. Patiently for two weeks the delegates listened to the evidence produced by the accusers and the accused, and then the vote was taken separately upon each specification, which resulted in finding the accused, H. B. Hartzler, guilty of the charges which had been preferred against him. The accused was absolutely empty-handed, that is, he was unable to produce one single proof to sustain the fearful accusations which he had made, whether against Bishop Esher, or his report, or the Board of Missions, or its Executive Committee, or other officials of the Church. The trial proved that the agitation carried on in the *Evangelical*

Messenger by its editor and his correspondents was absolutely without cause, utterly unjustifiable, and hence declared by the General Conference to have been a crime. To this day the Church has not recovered from that unholy crusade against its general officers and official bodies, and it may require a generation of time until it does.

Notwithstanding the serious nature of the charges of which H. B. Hartzler was found guilty, he was treated with great leniency by the General Conference. Had the law been enforced as it is found in our Discipline, he would have been deposed from office and expelled from the Church. There is no doubt that he had deserved such a sentence. The crime of which he was found guilty and the injury he had done would have fully justified, even demanded the extreme penalty. But he was only deposed from his office as editor of the *Evangelical Messenger*, thus dealing with him in the mildest manner possible. It was still hoped that leniency with the agitators would possibly after all have the effect of securing peace and rest, and prevent a schism.

When finally the business of the General Conference was finished, and the usual motion to authorize the Secretary to subscribe the names of the members to the proceedings as a token of acquiescence and obedience, in accordance with the directions of our Discipline, was pending, a considerable number of the delegates, for the first time in the history of the Church, voted "No." This, of course, made it necessary that the roll should be called, whereupon the following named delegates refused to sign the proceedings as the Discipline directs, namely, M. J. Carothers, U. F. Swengel, L. M. Boyer, T. Bach, I. M. Pines, C. W. Anthony, W. M. Stanford, E. B. Utt, W. E. Detweiler, J. D. Domer, and I. A. Rohland.

Probably the reproduction of an article written for the *Evangelical Messenger*, dated November 6, 1888, by the writer, entitled, "*What will the Harvest be?*" may be in place here:

"The sad scene at the close of the General Conference, when a large number of delegates, even several annual conference delegations, refused their signatures to the proceedings of that body, required by our Discipline, and by thus refusing served notice upon the Church that they would neither acquiesce in what had been done, nor obey the regulations which had been adopted, shattered all fond hopes. And when immediately after the General Conference the editor, deposed from his office by that body, was elected as editor of an independent paper, not in the sense of an independent Christian weekly intended for general circulation among the various Christian denominations, but as an independent Church paper for our Church, assuming our name by misnaming itself *Evangelical*, the last ray of hope for peace and harmony vanished. The notice not to acquiesce in the proceedings in nor obey the regulations of General Conference was put into practice. The seed of dissension which had been sown during the past years had now ripened into its first harvest, namely into organized opposition against the publishing interests of our Church, and the tendency of the paper published by this organization fixed in direct opposition to the government of our Church. Before that, Rev. H. B. Hartzler stood alone, I mean alone in so far that there was no organization supporting his rebellion, at least no known public organization. What all may have been done ' confidentially ' is known to God only, although a good many links in the chain are known to some of us also, and probably more than some people are aware of, and the missing ones may yet be discovered. However, now things have assumed a different aspect. Rev. H. B. Hartzler and his associates are now the mouth-pieces of an incorporated organization, and his paper the organ of that organization. Hence the opposition is now organized, and *most certainly not without some purpose or end in view.* That special purpose can not be simply to print religious articles which may be written by its editors and correspondents, for all these would have had room in our own weeklies and monthlies. That special purpose was not the making of money. Its projectors are too shrewd to undertake such a business for that object.

It can have no other purpose than to continue to pursue the same end which was not accomplished while controlling our own English paper, with only this difference, that the swath if possible shall be wider.

"What will the harvest be? Whatsoever a man soweth, that shall he also reap. The harvest will be the same in kind with the seed which has been sown. We can judge the future only by the past, and if that is a correct indication, then the chasm will become broader and deeper, until the possibility of its being bridged must be abandoned by the most hopeful. There is no reasonable doubt that nearly all the same persons who refused to sign their signatures to the proceedings of the late General Conference will be re-elected delegates to the next General Conference. *Will the General Conference recognize them as such? Can it recognize them as such, while they have openly declared they will not abide by its decisions and will not submit to its arrangements?* Either the authority and the dignity of the General Conference, and with it all lawful authority in our Church, must be set aside, and set aside for all the future, and all the authority of law and government be at an end among us; or those who refused to assent to the proceedings of that body and submit to its provisions, must acknowledge their error, and ask for an opportunity and the privilege of correcting their grave mistake, but if what some of us were compelled to hear at our annual Board meetings is a correct index in that direction, this latter course will not be adopted. Under these circumstances does not every intelligent reader see what the harvest will be?

"If these same persons are re-elected as delegates, of which there is very little doubt, if they still live, and will not entertain the thought of submission, and sign the proceedings of our last General Conference, held in Buffalo, N. Y., what other course is left them but to withdraw from the next? The stake was driven in before they left Buffalo, and they will find it standing upon their return where they drove it by their own deliberate action. Only those who placed the obstruction at the door upon going away can remove it. I most sincerely hope I may be mistaken, and that they will come and acknowledge their mistake, and remove the bar from the door, by doing what they should have done at Buffalo, namely sign the proceedings, provided, of course, the General Conference will grant them the privilege of repentance after continuing in their course for four years.

"Then will the hour have come when every other delegate must choose whether he will remain with the Evangelical Association, or whether he will go with ———. Then will the 'loyalty' and the 'devotion' of everyone be put to a practical test. That will be the hour of decision. These things are before us, and it would be folly to close our eyes against them, or try to make the impression that all is serene and everything lovely when it is not true. In fact it would be hypocrisy to say peace where there is no peace, and hypocrisy is a thing all honest people despise.

"However, let it be remembered that should the catastrophe be inevitable, that a number of delegates will withdraw from the next General Conference, their action would not take the conferences they represent out of our Church. Not by any means. Nor even would the withdrawal of the majority from any annual conference carry out the conference as such. Those remaining would be the ——— conference of the Evangelical Association. So, also, those remaining of our local societies would be the society holding the Church property and worship in it. Those going would have to commence anew in every particular, name, discipline, property, and everything else. The fathers of our Church built upon solid ground. They have given us a liberal form of Church government, yet a strong government, making us a Church one and inseparable. Individuals always maintain and have their right of an individual choice, but the Church is one.

"I know I shall be severely censured for writing these things, but that shall not molest me. Facts are facts, and truth is truth. We are not dealing, to use the language of President

Cleveland, 'with a theory, but with a condition.' This condition and these facts confront us. I believe it to be my duty, before God and the Church I love, to sound the note of warning, and not remain silent when dangers surround us, but clearly state the case just as it is. In my humble opinion the day is not far distant when everyone must choose whether he will remain with our beloved Church, in which we have been spiritually born and nurtured, and in which there are so many fond and gracious memories, or go with an element or faction, either to some other denomination, or in this age of the world organize a new denomination and commence a new struggle for life and existence."

How roundly the writer was abused in the *Evangelical* and elsewhere by the seceders for exposing their plans is well known, and yet how minutely have the predicted events come to pass! With only this difference that instead of coming to the General Conference of our Church and then withdrawing in a body, when not allowed to dictate its policy and work, and holding their own separate "conference," they did not even come to the General Conference of the Evangelical Association, or make the least attempt to adjust the differences, but at once went off by themselves more than six hundred miles away from where the General Conference had been appointed, and held a 'conference' of their own. The majority of the leaders of this movement very well knew they had disqualified themselves by open acts of rebellion from ever again sitting in the General Conference of our Church unless they repented and obligated themselves to obey the Discipline of the Church : hence this move on their part, by which they split the Church wide open. At present in some places they still claim to be the Evangelical Association, while at others, as for instance in Illinois, they have set up a new Church under a different name, in Oregon the courts have compelled them to adopt still another name, and the time has come "when everyone must choose whether he will remain with our beloved Church in which he has been spiritually born," or unite with this "new denomination," at the head of which stands Rudolph Dubs, who has been deposed from the office of the ministry and expelled from the Church for immorality, a sentence pronounced by the Supreme Court of the Church to which he formerly belonged, and confirmed and enforced by the Supreme Court of the State of Illinois, of which he is a citizen.

The first open act of rebellion against the Church was in the shape of a so-called protest offered in the General Conference in Buffalo after the trial of H. B. Hartzler was over, protesting against any sentence being passed upon the accused after he had been found guilty. Had the "protest" been drawn up in proper language, setting forth reasons why the Conference should not take any further action, it might probably have been admissible, although it is a question whether any protest is admissible in the highest executive and judicial body of a Church. But this "protest" was an open declaration of nullification and war. While it protested against the trial of one of the General Conference members as not having been legal, it condemned another member not only without any trial whatever, but even without charges or notice of charges. Hence it was ruled out of order by the Chair. *From this ruling of the presiding Bishop no appeal was taken*, consequently no record could appear in the proceedings of the Conference of this treasonable act.

The second open act of rebellion was a refusal to sign the proceedings of the General Conference of 1887. This has already been referred to. Refusing to sign the proceedings "as a token of acquiescence and obedience" as the Discipline requires, was of course giving notice to the Church that they would not submit to what had been done.

The third open act of rebellion was the formation of a stock company for the purpose of publishing an independent paper in Harrisburg, Pa., in opposition to the regular official papers of the Church, and appointing as the editor of this paper Rev. H. B. Hartzler, who had been deposed for making war upon the Church. The notice not to submit "to the regulations of this Association," as instituted by its Supreme Court, by refusing to sign the proceedings as a token of acquiescence and obedience was now carried out. In this rebellious act not only such as had given the notice above referred to participated, but quite a number even of those who had pledged their word and honor to "acquiesce and obey" became not only shareholders in this corporation of opposition, but active members of its board of directors and executive committee, and associates in the work, bringing if possible still more infamy upon themselves.

However, this is not all. Even four of the persons elected at this General Conference of 1887 as members of the Board of Publication of our Publishing House in Cleveland were in full sympathy with this opposition sheet, and one of them at least, Rev. D. B. Byers, an active correspondent of the same, hence in league with a corporation organized specifically to operate against the interests of the business which they were elected to aid in managing in the interest of the Church! And one of the four was even a Bishop of the Church, who drew his support from the Publishing House he was secretly undermining, and who was aiding wherever and whenever he could an opposition concern. That this person was Rudolph Dubs of Cleveland, O., goes for the saying; of this fact the evidence is abundantly in our possession. In connection it may be in place to mention an incident which has been used by Dubs in his own interests, simply because he has perverted the facts. At a meeting of the Executive Committee of the Board of Publication consisting of the three Bishops, held in the Publishing House in Cleveland, O., in the presence of the Publishers, Revs. M. Lauer and H. Mattill, the financial interests of the Publishing House were discussed, and methods suggested how best to keep up our subscription lists, in view of the opposition by a pretty large portion of the ministers of the Church, represented by the concern at Harrisburg, Pa., and further the interests of the business in general. The methods of the opposition and their efforts to cut down the subscription lists of our periodicals were also spoken of. The situation was fully realized. We knew it would require an earnest and united effort of all who stood by the actions of the Buffalo General Conference to carry the House successfully through the crisis which was upon us. The Publishers suggested that unanimity among the Bishops on this point would go very far in this respect. The writer then very earnestly appealed to Bishop Dubs to use his influence personally and officially for the business interests of the Publishing House, stating that he specially had influence with the opposition element, adding that as a Bishop it was his duty to stand up for the Church and her interests. Finally Bishop Esher also addressed himself to Bishop Dubs pleading with him that at such a juncture and crisis in the Church, when not only her financial interests, but the very life of the Church was at stake, he ought as one of the chief pastors stand by his colleagues, and the other General Conference officers. After Bishop Esher had thus spoken the writer appealed to Dubs again in language which could not be misunderstood. The only answer either of us received was a statement to the effect that if any of us wanted to go to Dayton, O., where the Board of Missions was to meet, we could get reduced rates by calling at such and such a place, and then left the room!

Perhaps the pretext for starting an opposition paper at Harrisburg, Pa., should also receive some attention. The opposition has said the *Evangelical* was called into existence because the newly elected editor of the *Messenger*, Rev. S. P. Spreng, had refused to publish articles written by the Dubs faction. No more glaring falsehood was circulated by this element in our difficulties than this, and nothing could be more unjust to the new Editor. The arrangements for publishing the *Evangelical* were made before the General Conference had adjourned, before the Dubs delegates left Buffalo. The prospectus of that paper was published ere a single one of these gentlemen had written a communication for the *Messenger* and forwarded it to the newly elected editor, hence the utter falsity of their statements.

During the Spring of 1889 the rumors that Bishop Dubs was telling the untruth in the statements he had made that he had not been invited either by Rev. C. K. Fehr or Rev. S. C. Breyfogel, then Presiding Elders in the East Pa. Conference, were spoken of very freely. Mention was also made of a letter in the hand-writing of Bishop Dubs, but signed anonymously, on this wise, "my name, is no name," in which he reflected very seriously upon his colleagues and the other General Conference officers, and which plainly indicated his attitude in the conflict which had been forced upon the Church. Hence Bishop Esher and the writer forcibly realized that things could not go on in this way without at least making an effort to right them. Moreover the agitation caused by the opposition paper published in Harrisburg, Pa., and other publications assailed the General Conference of 1887, alleging that it had been a "packed" body etc., impressed upon us as chief pastors of the Church the duty of speaking to our colleague personally and if possible agreeing upon a pastoral address to allay the excitement, and in some measure restore confidence. Accordingly a meeting of the Bishops was appointed in Chicago at a time when it was known Bishop Dubs would pass through that city, thus making it possible to meet without incurring extra expense or much loss of time. Due notice had been given each of the Bishops in ample time. Two of the Bishops met at the time and place appointed, but the third came not. Next day Bishop Esher received a letter from Bishop Dubs, mailed at Toledo, O., saying that he did not think a meeting of the Bishops to be important, and he had therefore passed through Chicago without stopping! The Church agitated and excited from centre to circumference, and yet of no importance in Dubs' opinion for its chief pastors even to have a meeting and consult together!

The writer was to start for Europe a week later, and as we considered an episcopal meeting before that simply a necessity, the writer at the instance of Bishop Esher, who was our chairman, notified Bishop Dubs that an episcopal meeting would now be held on the following Saturday at 9 A. M. in Bishop Esher's house. In this letter the reasons were also stated why we considered a meeting absolutely necessary, stating among other things the new rumors affecting his veracity, which were being circulated (of which the writer had already apprised Dubs in a personal letter months before). The train from Cleveland arrived in Chicago at 7:35 A. M. The meeting was called at 9 A. M. Bishop Dubs came to Bishop Esher's house where the meeting was called *after dinner*, and then he pretended to be in a great hurry, saying he wanted to go to the North side to visit his son, and must leave in the evening for his appointment in Michigan. It was evident to both of us that it was a studied effort on the part of Bishop Dubs to defeat any effort at adjustment and settlement of the difficulties. There were important matters connected with affairs in Japan to be attended too. These and other matters were discussed and arranged. Then the matter of a pastoral address was discussed, and the address prepared by Bishop Esher, at the suggestion of his colleagues at a previous meeting was read, but Dubs refused to sign it, although he did not point out anything objectionable; and so the address was never published.

The address was the following:

THE PROPOSED EPISCOPAL ADDRESS.

Whereas, The general superintendency of the Evangelical Association and of all her churches, institutions, and general affairs has been imposed upon us the undersigned as a solemn duty, together with all the grave responsibilities for the faithful performance of this duty: knowing also that the welfare of our Church is immeasurably dependent upon such faithful performance of this duty; and further, as is well known, a serious disturbance having arisen in our Church which has already caused great offence and much injury and threatens still greater harm, we are therefore impelled by a sense of duty as well as by our concern for our Church and her interests to address the following, in the name of our Lord Jesus Christ, to the preachers and members of the Evangelical Association:

The Evangelical Association is a church communion thoroughly well organized in accordance with the divine word and order. Her economy came into existence through servants of the Lord divinely called and guided. This organization, therefore, exists by divine right and is to be regarded and obeyed with reverential submission and sacred fidelity by all such as have submitted themselves to it. This duty of submission and obedience on the part of all who stand in connection with the Evangelical Association has been voluntarily assumed and is therefore unconditionally binding as long as they continue in such relationship.

The Discipline of the Evangelical Association is her constitution and her ecclesiastical law. The entire Church with all that belongs to it, including every officer, preacher, and member, exists under this law.

Under the Discipline the General Conference is the supreme power in the Evangelical Association. In it the entire Church is represented. This Conference in turn is represented in the Boards appointed by it in accordance with an existing right. These Boards act, in the name of and in accordance with the instructions given and authority conferred by the General Conference, during the intervals of its quadrennial sessions, managing the general institutions and affairs of the Church. All these boards, general institutions and affairs, as well as the appointed officers of the Church are subject to the control and under the supervision of the General Conference.

All the determinations of the General Conference, formed in accordance with the Discipline, are legally binding. In like manner all the regulations of these various boards made in accordance with the Discipline and the instructions of the General Conference are valid and binding until altered or abolished. The General Conference alone has power to judge of the regularity of its own proceedings.

Reverent submission, obedience, fidelity and a proper regard for the authorities of the Church and her decisions, for the various institutions, and above all for the Discipline of the Church itself—these are the characteristics of true Church fidelity as well as the indispensable conditions of good order, peace and prosperity, of the very honor and strength of the Church. On the contrary a disregard of these qualities is disloyalty to the Church, a reproach upon her name and an offence against her life and her divine Lord. But an uprising against the Church in an effort to injure her on the part of those who still stand in her connection can only be designated as rebellion.

The validity of our Discipline up to the present stands unimpeached inasmuch as everything which it contains, without exception, has been incorporated in a lawful manner. Never before did the General Conference in its transactions act with greater caution nor adhere with closer fidelity to the Discipline of the Church than at its recent session, in 1887. In consequence of this its transactions, without exception, stand in closest accord with the Church polity recognized by the Evangelical Association.

Our boards also have in these later years adhered, if possible, with a greater degree of accuracy to the law of the Church and observed more carefully their instructions than formerly. Never before has the record of our general church administration in all its parts been kept with greater fidelity and in closer conformity to law and order. The general institutions and affairs of our Church in these later years have been managed with tact, diligence and fidelity, in consequence of which these institutions are enjoying great peace and prosperity. While the Church owes to her servants engaged in these institutions a proper recognition, to God, from whom comes the increase, are due devout thanksgivings and adoration. Never was there manifest in the Church a deeper interest and a more zealous participation in these institutions; never were they more liberally supported by the prayers and gifts of our preachers and people than at present. This general support, wrought by the Holy Spirit, is visibly becoming stronger and more cordial. To all this we your overseers bear witness with great confidence in God and with joyous thanksgivings.

It is only in those localities where the aforementioned disturbance has entered congregations that this participation in and consequent support of our institutions has measurably diminished and in some instances altogether disappeared.

Through improper attacks made upon the Boards and general officers of the Church and upon their official acts by the Editor of the *Evangelical Messenger* for a number of years, this disturbance finally culminated in an outbreak.

The disturbance consists, in the main, in the unreasonable and unrighteous onslaughts which the aforementioned Editor made and which he continued to make with increasing vehemence, in spite of repeated admonitions, resulting in the serious distraction of the Church for a long time; in the antagonism, an antagonism growing out of the foregoing, of a number of delegates to our last General Conference (in 1887) and their opposition to a part of its proceedings; in the fact that a number of the delegates not only refused to sign the proceedings in accordance with the instructions of the Discipline, but even put themselves upon record as opposed to such an act, thereby making themselves guilty of a refusual to fulfill their solemn vows of obedience, and guilty moreover of an actual uprising against the Discipline and against the Church itself.

This disturbance consists further in the unauthorized publication and dissemination of a weekly periodical pretending to be a Church paper. A Church paper can be lawfully published only by direction of the General Conference. The right of any one to publish a paper for himself is not disputed, nevertheless the publication of a paper with the utterances of the aforementioned one by ministers and members of the Evangelical Association, without direction of General Conference, unauthorized in every sense, is a disregard for the authority of the Church and an invasion of the order and affairs of the Church. And inasmuch as this paper antagonizes the regular Church organs, spreading many false reports and unfounded accusations and making many attacks upon the boards and officers of the Church, thereby disturbing the peace of the Church, dishonoring her good name, injuring her institutions and in short carrying on a rebellion against the Church, a sense of duty constrains us to exhort our preachers and members to offer no open doors to this false accuser of the brethren and disturber of our peace, and not to make themselves partakers of this sin. We would remind those who have assisted in the publication and dissemination of this paper, thereby injuring the circulation of our Church papers, that they make themselves guilty not only of a serious violation of their vows of fidelity to the Church, but of actual perfidy and rebellion against the Churb in whose service they pretend to stand.

A further significant phase of this movement is to be found in the transactions of several Annual Conferences directed against certain proceedings of the General Conference under whose sovereignty they stand, thereby revolting against the General Conference itself and assuming an attitude which would necessarily lead to a dissolution of our Church organization. The most significant fact, however, in this connection is the justification by these conferences of the act of certain delegates, who in defiance of the Church Discipline, expressly declared themselves as opposed to the signing of the proceedings of General Conference. By these overt acts the law and order of the Church were totally disregarded, and serious disturbance and schism introduced. In fact by these proceedings disobedience to the General Conference and the Church Discipline were actully approved and defended. We urge these conferences to take these particular proceedings into earnest reconsideration and to rescind them.

Of similar significance are the transactions of certain Annual Conferences relative to the alleged state of the Church and the conduct of some of the general officers of the Church. In these transactions the law and the rights of the Evangelical Association are injured, for the General Conference alone is authorized to speak on the state of the Church within the scope in which it was attempted by these Annual Conferences; it alone has rightful jurisdiction over the boards and general officers of the Church. Therefore, in accusing general officers of the Church of grave offences and in publicly censuring—while acting in a judicial capacity—these brethren, these Annual Conferences made themselves guilty of a serious disregard of our Discipline and Church authority. And this they did without the knowledge of these general officers, to say nothing of the right of a hearing. It must be remembered that such a censure is regarded by our Discipline as a punishment. By these means they pleaded the cause of and rendered great aid to this distracting movement in our Church.

Another exhibition of their contempt for the highest authority of the Church and its declared will, as well as of biblical and therefore divine right, is the attempt to deprive some of our Annual Conferences of their rights, in part at least, in our College at Naperville, whereby they not only deliberately and persistently acted in direct opposition to an express provision of the General Conference, but whereby a divine command, right and righteousness were trodden under foot. It is with pain and deep regret that we mention this fact, a fact which stands in such close connection with the injurious agitation in our Church, one which is so deeply humiliating to us as a Church and on account of which the name of the Lord is reviled in the world and we are put to shame before unbelievers. We rejoice, however, and thank God that, by his help, this base attempt to pervert the right has been signally overthrown. We also heartily rejoice in the firm sense of right which our laymen entertain on this subject and to which they have given such emphatic expression.

We would mention also, although we do it with a feeling of shame and with bitter sorrow, the report so persistently circulated that there exists in our Church a secret society (with the senior Bishop as its head!) having evil purposes in view. That this report has had its source in the fountain of lies was evident from the beginning. That this report has brought dishonor upon the fair name of our Church and that those who originated it and encouraged its circulation had an evil purpose are facts equally well known. It is a further clear proof of the evil designs of the disturbing element in our Church and with which this slanderous report is so closely allied. We deplore the fact that our honorable church bodies felt themselves necessitated to condescend to an investigation of the base affair, but comfort ourselves with the prospect that the disgrace of this outrage will finally fix itself upon its originators and abettors alone.

The aforementioned instances, together with many others, of disregard for our discipline and order, of revolt against the authorities of the Church and of a transgression of the divine order, have created a situation of the most serious character. This situation we desire to meet in such a manner as will effectually allay the injurious agitation and restore peace throughout all the borders of the Church. For the accomplishment of this, there is necessary above all else a radical separation from everything that is ungodly and a firm adherence to the divine Word and order. In addition to this an unconditional adherence to the law and regulations of our Church is of great importance. It is simply a question of life and death for our Church.

To overlook the aforenamed offences or to excuse those who have made themselves guilty is out of the question. The Church has been guilty of no wrong and therefore cannot enter upon any compromise with such as have violated her order or transgressed her laws. Such a compromise would be an offence against her own life, veritable self destruction, whereas a firm adherence to her divine order will secure a peaceful and prosperous future. Our Church is organized in accordance with the Word of God, an organism which dare not sacrifice itself to the purposes of self seeking persons; it belongs to Christ. For such as have made themselves guilty of the aforesaid offences there remains only, according to God's Word, a choice between a suitable and adequate reformation or a separation from the Church. In the name of the Lord Jesus Christ we exhort them to reform and to return to a genuine church loyalty; but that in the event they reject this then for the peace of the Church to take that step which a sense of honor should itself dictate to them.

We conclude with the following additional remarks:

1. Above all else, let each one earnestly strive to be in a right state of grace, separate from the world, walking in Christian self-denial according to the mind and example of Jesus Christ and the holy commandments of our God.

2. We exhort the preachers and congregational officers of the Church to see to it that our congregations are found in a true state of grace, in godliness, and in good works, that they become edified

more and more in holiness before God, that our regulations be jointly upheld, and that our Church Discipline be enforced in accordance with the Word of God. Thus will not only the churches be presented to Christ the Lord in purity and in blamelessness, but also became established in a beautiful Christian order and in church loyalty, and be advanced unto a vigorous church maturity. On the contrary, superficiality in the Christian life and in the administration of the affairs of the congregations will open wide the door to all manner of disorder.

3. Let us adhere, with faithful insistance, to our pure biblical doctrines of experimental religion, the consciousness of divine sonship, holiness of heart and blamelessness of life according to the Word of God and by faith in Jesus. Let us as preachers and officials confirm these doctrines by our own life and conduct in the truth as before God. The fact that in a number of places a serious relaxation in these matters has taken place constrains us all the more to bring this highly important subject to your thoughtful attention.

4. With reverence for the Word of God let us adjust according to its precepts all our personal life, our family life, and our congregational life. Him who has the fear of God's Word in his heart will God honor and bless.

5. Let us with all fidelity hold fast to the admirable order of our Church, honoring her laws with obedience, faithfully serving the Lord in the fellowship of the Spirit and in the communion of saints unto the inner edification and outer prosperity of the Evangelical Association.

If these exhortations of your chief shepherds be taken to heart then shall the Spirit's gracious operations in our Church effectually quench this disturbing agitation and that peace which is the fruit of righteousness and which is preserved in true holiness will be restored. Any other peace we do not want; for the Evangelical Association there is no other.

We exhort to a continuance in prayer. Our help is the name of the Lord who made heaven and earth. Let us hold fast to His Word and walk faithfully in His truth. In Him we trust.

YOUR BRETHREN IN CHRIST.

Then the writer called attention to the rumors above mentioned affecting the veracity of Bishop Dubs. His answer was that he absolutely refused to say anything about those things and would give no explanation whatever. The writer then also charged Bishop Dubs with writing an anonymous letter reflecting upon his colleagues and other General Conference officers. This he denied in strong and positive language, although the letter is in existence and in our possession, thus making himself guilty of another falsehood to hide the cowardly course he was pursuing. And thus we parted. A few days later the writer started for Europe, and R. Dubs continued to perform the functions of his office, knowing that he was charged with willful and even malicious falsehood, yet refusing to even make an explanation! He had been so frequently confronted with this detestable sin that it apparently made very little impression upon him. But how in the face of these facts can his colleagues be charged with seeking his overthrow when they tried their utmost to save him, and why charge them with tyranny, when they exercised forbearance and leniency for years, for the exercising of which they are now censured? Up to the time when these things here chronicled occurred, Bishop Esher and the writer informed Bishop Dubs, as our Discipline and the Word of God directs, of the rumors affecting his moral character, again and again. This was done without at any time receiving any satisfactory explanation from him, or without leading to any action on his part to adjust the charges against him with the parties from whom they came. The writer resolved when parting with Bishop Dubs at the meeting above referred to that his duty towards the latter in that respect had been fully done, and that if such reports would come to him in the future some other course would be pursued which should compel him or his accusers to meet the accusations. Hence, when during the writer's visit in Europe, he was informed of the manner in which Dubs had defrauded the European conferences out of their proper representation in the General Conference of 1887, and knowing that this was done in the interests of his party, for political purposes, the writer so stated it in his correspondence in the Church papers without, however, directly mentioning Dubs' name. For the same reason when the writer was directly and reliably informed of Dubs' outrageously indecent conduct towards a sister, he made it known without first speaking to Dubs. This latter accusation against him has been proven by direct testimony. The first accusation of defrauding European conferences was proven later to be much worse than it had been originally stated. He had defrauded the Germany and Switzerland Conferences out of their legal representation by glaringly untruthful statements and by threats and intimidations; especially was this the case in the Switzerland Conference. Bishop Dubs replied to the statement made by the writer, in which he made matters still worse. In order to cover up the falsehoods he had told the conferences from the chair as their president, he again prevaricated, and in every article he wrote got deeper into the mire. Bishop Dubs now not only stood charged with falsehood privately, but he stood charged and convicted by the overwhelming testimony of about forty ministers, before the entire Church, in its official organs, with deliberate falsehood! Nor was this all. Bishop Dubs in his defense, which he wrote in the Church papers, had charged Rev. M. Pfitzinger and Mr. E. B. Esher with falsifying a certain telegram, and these in a statement in the *Botschafter* also clearly convicted him of falsehood and slander. *And yet although he thus stood charged before the entire Church, in its official papers, he continued in the performance of his official duties. Even when finally action was taken, he tried to evade an examination by three elders, and when the trial was instituted and held, where his honor and his all was at stake, he ran away from it on a most trivial pretext.*

In October, 1889, at an Episcopal meeting held in Rev. M. Lauer's house, Bishop Dubs' colleagues again and for the last time called his attention to the serious accusations which had been made against him. Bishop Esher addressed Bishop Dubs in his characteristically mild but firm manner. The writer once again repeated to Dubs the category of sins with which he stood charged in plain and unvarnished terms, declaring that something must be done to have these matters cleared up. Again he evaded us. A certain political leader, whom he was anxious to hear, had been advertised to speak in Cleveland that evening, hence he had no time to talk these things over any longer, and wanted to hasten away. A bishop of the Evangelical Association is being privately and publicly charged with the most serious crimes. The Church is in a state of excitement throughout its entire borders about these and other matters. Its chief pastors, whose duty it is to see that everything is done in accordance with the Word of God, and who should certainly have an interest in the welfare of the Church, if anybody has, have a meeting, *but one of them is so utterly indifferent to all these things that to attend a political meeting is to him of greater importance than to discuss, and if possible find a way out of the grave situation in which we were as a Church in the Fall of 1889!* While night and day earnest hearts were throbbing for the welfare of the Church, and everywhere loyal Evangelical ministers and members are anxiously inquiring, "What is going to be the outcome?" "Where will these things end?" this bishop of the Church is more concerned in a political meeting than in a discussion of the situation, and in discovering some plan to avert ruin and disaster. This, indeed, had been his course for years. He never had "time" to thoroughly inquire into existing difficulties, and when he could frame no excuse then he treated his colleagues with contempt and abruptly went away from their presence. Upon the contrary, he always found it convenient to stop over in Chicago to consult with the "Illinois Conference ring." At Buffalo, during the General Conference, that earnest period of the history of our Church, he could at no time find it convenient to consult with his colleagues, but every day he and his associates in ecclesiastical politics found time to consult together. The day before he made his sensational and entirely undisciplinary ruling in reference to the charges which had been preferred against H. B. Hartzler, he and about twenty others had a meeting in which Hartzler's objections to the manner and form of the specifications were presented and discussed, and a plan of action agreed upon. It was therefore unnecessary for H. B. Hartzler to argue his objections before the chairman who was to decide upon the questions at issue. He had done that in a private circle the day before, and knowing how the chair would rule, he could submit his case without argument. This secret conclave afforded Dubs time to write out a lengthy opinion, *and argue Hartzler's case from the chair*. As an appeal had to be taken under the rules without debate, Dubs and his associates also knew there would be no opportunity to answer the sophistries he presented, and thus their purpose of defeating an investigation would be accomplished. More especially if the vote on the appeal from the ruling of the chair would be taken by ballot, which they had also agreed upon at their conclave. Who knows whether the adroitly laid plan had not succeeded had not the mover of the appeal preceeded this motion with a brief preamble answering the sophistries with a few briefly stated facts?

However, it may be proper to return to the last Episcopal meeting at which Bishop Dubs was present, held in Rev. M. Lauer's house and referred to above. Notwithstanding his hurry to get away to hear some political speaker, we compelled him to remain long enough to hear us. In a speech of probably twenty minutes the writer rehearsed the crimes with which he stood charged in vigorous and very plain language. During this time Dubs covered his face with the writing pad he had been using as secretary of the Board. The only reply we received in answer to the long category was that the statement made by Rev. C. K. Fehr that he had invited him to his camp-meetings was untrue. We replied by saying that on the following Tuesday (this was on Saturday evening) we would meet Bro. Fehr at the annual meeting of the Trustees of the Orphan Home at Flat Rock, O., and in his presence the matter should be talked over. *However, Dubs had no time to attend that meeting on the following Tuesday, although he was at home in Cleveland.* After the writer had finished and Dubs had made the reply. above given, Bishop Esher called Bishop Dubs' attention to the letter he (Esher) had written to the laymen's convention in Chicago in reference to the confession Dubs had made in the writer's home in Allentown, Pa., in 1883, that he (Dubs) had entered upon his Episcopal career with the fixed purpose of putting Bishop Esher down, demanding to know whether he had not correctly stated what had taken place at that meeting. In our presence Bishop Dubs did not have the moral courage to deny the correctness of the statement Bishop Esher had made ; not a single word. Why ? Because he knew it was correct and true in every word and sentence. In our absence he has attempted to summon courage indirectly to deny the correctness of our statements. Of course, in view of everything else he has been capable of, this occasions but little surprise. After what has been stated, the reader will not be surprised to find that finally formal charges were presented against Bishop Dubs, and proceedings taken in accordance with our Discipline.

CHAPTER VIII.

The Trial and Conviction of Bishop Dubs.

After every effort had failed to prevail upon Bishop Dubs if possible to explain and adjust matters in some manner satisfactory to the Church, charges were drawn up, and in accordance with our disciplinary provisions he was waited upon by three elders who, after considerable difficulty, finally heard him, and being convinced of his guilt, notwithstanding his explanations, instituted a trial conference, which convened in Cleveland, Ohio, on the 18th of February, 1890. It required considerable courage on the part of the three elders, who had waited upon him, to proceed, as he did his utmost to intimidate them by all manner of threats. He not only attempted to intimidate the three elders, but also some of the witnesses. Especially was this the case with Rev. R. Mott, who was put to considerable expense to refute the slander Dubs tried to fasten upon him in order to cover up his own sins. However, the evidence presented by Bro. Mott not only fully vindicated him but uncovered Dubs' character and purposes more fully.

When the trial conference met it first adopted a series of business rules for its own guidance and protection, and also to insure protection to and guarantee the rights of all concerned. It also made arrangements, in view of the far-reaching character of its work, for the appointment of a stenographer, an elder of our own Church. One of the business rules adopted was that no one who was not an elder in the Church would be permitted to be present. This rule is in harmony with the business rules of the General Conference. Another rule forbade any one to appear as counsel who was not a member of our Church either for the accused or the accusers.

When the trial conference was ready to proceed the accused demanded the right to appoint two stenographers who were not members of our Church. This demand being in conflict with the rules adopted by the trial conference could not be granted, especially in view that the court had already made provisions for a full stenographic report, with the agreement and understanding that all concerned should have the right to refer to the official record made by the stenographer at any time during the course of the trial. *This unlawful demand of the accused not being granted he withdrew from the conference.*

In the first instance he had done his utmost to evade an examination by the three elders. When this failed he attempted to deter them from further proceedings by intimidation, and then when his unreasonable and illegal demands were not complied with he left the conference, hoping doubtless thereby to prevent it from proceeding with the trial. At all events the air was full of threatenings as to what all Dubs would do if the trial conference proceeded. His last dollar, it was said, would be spent to secure justice in the courts, etc. It is certain he did consult an attorney in reference to the matter who gave him the sensible advice to go and stand his trial like a man. Dubs, however, knowing what evidence could be produced against him, wanted no trial, hence the advice of his counsel was not followed.

As so much ado has been made concerning the fact that Mr. E. B. Esher, a lay member of the Church, was permitted to be present during the trial, and Rev. C. N. Dubs, a son of Bishop Dubs, and a deacon in the Church, was not admitted, a brief statement may be necessary. Rev. M. Pfitzinger, one of the accusers, had chosen Bro. Esher as one of his counsel, as he had a right to do, and had so informed the trial conference, for which reason he was permitted to be present. Bishop Dubs made no request to have his son admitted, consequently the conference knew nothing of his presence in the basement of the church, nor of any desire on his part to be present. Had Dubs made known his desire to have his son present, there is no doubt the request would have been readily granted. Why accuse the trial conference of refusing a request which was never made either by Bishop Dubs or his son Newton? Moreover, the writer is of the opinion that had Dubs remained and stood his trial " like a man," as his counsel advised, he would never have asked to have his son Newton to be present. Bishop Dubs expected that a great deal more of his unchaste conduct would be exposed than was actually done, and he did not want to have his son hear his father's shame. Dubs knew that there was at least one person present at that trial to whom he had confidentially related how he had visited *alone* the "can-cans" and other low resorts in Paris when on his first Episcopal visit to Europe. He also knew that there were persons there who knew of the evening walks he had taken with a certain woman, who was not his wife, in sparsely settled portions of Chicago, and also that he had ridden in a closed carriage after ten o'clock at night for several miles with a woman who was not his wife, as well as a number of other damaging rumors affecting his chastity, which were not uncovered. Bishop Dubs did not ask to have his son present at all and he did not want him present, but because the person stationed at the door in order to see that the rules of the conference were carried out told Bishop Dubs' son that under the rules he could not be admitted, it furnished the rebellious element with an occasion to make capital for themselves.

This trial conference of fifteen ministers, none of whom, probably, had been a minister for less than twenty years, and some of them for forty years, seven of them presiding elders at the time, four of them ex-presiding elders, representing ten different Annual Conferences, not only men of ripe experience, but also representative men of the Church, respected as such at home and abroad. After hearing the evidence, the trial conference voted by ballot on each specification separately, finding the accused guilty of every specification, and guilty of the charges of immorality, and suspended him from his office as Bishop and minister until the next General Conference.

The writer does not consider it at all necessary to review this trial or the evidence presented. The Church has been informed concerning the same, and the General Conference at its subsequent session in Indianapolis, Ind., after a thorough investigation of the whole matter, unanimously confirmed and ratified the proceedings, deposing the accused R. Dubs, from the office as Bishop and minister and expelling him from the Church.

There is one point, however, which in the opinion of the writer has at no time received the attention its heinousness demands. It alone exposes Dubs' character, and would in itself be fully sufficient to justify the verdict against him. It is contained in specification 5, b, and refers to Dubs' conduct in reference to a young minister in the New York Conference. This young man had accused Dubs in a letter he wrote to a friend (names need not be given as their absence changes no facts), of grossly improper conduct towards a married woman. Under date of Feb. 28, 1884, the writer of this book, called Dubs' attention to this ugly accusation, *as well as others of a similar character*. On the 7th of May following Dubs answered in a letter, saying he had seen the young minister in question, and after explaining to him his (Dubs) intimacy with the family for twenty years, he (the young minister) was satisfied with Dubs' explanation. The writer hereof considered it very strange at the time, that a father of a family, a minister, and even a Bishop of our Church should not insist that the person who had made such a serious accusation in writing must himself recall the same, and state the facts in the case. The writer believed he had done his duty in the matter and would leave it where it was. Later on in the course of events, rumors came to the writer's ears, that the young minister in question, denied the truthfulness of Dubs' statement regarding his interview with Dubs. Hence further inquiries were made. In a statement made by the minister in question, in his own handwriting occurs the following passage: "Dubs said to me, well I will write to the brother and tell him that I had an interview with you in reference to this matter, and that my explanation was satisfactory, but I answered him No." After receiving this statement from this young minister, and knowing that he was to be ordained an elder in the Church at the session of the New York Conference, at which Bishop Dubs was to preside, the writer addressed another letter to Dubs informing him of what the young minister had written concerning their interview, adding, "one of you deliberately lies." The conference session was held. The conference ignorant of all these things voted the young man his ordination. On the Sabbath of the conference, during the ordination services, Bishop Rudolph Dubs read from our Discipline as follows: "Brethren, these are the persons whom we purpose, God willing, this day to ordain elders; for after due examination we find naught to the contrary, but that they are lawfully called to this function and ministry, and that they are persons meet for the same. But if there be any of you who knows of any crime or impediment for which he ought not be admitted to this office, let him come forth in the name of God, and state what such crime or impediment is." After reading this challenge at the altar of God, Bishop Rudolph Dubs lays his hands on the young man's head and ordains him to the highest order in our Church—ordains a man who over his own signature had accused the Bishop of grossly improper conduct toward a married woman, and who had never retracted the accusation, and who furthermore over his own signature declared the Bishop guilty of deliberate falsehood, and the Bishop knows it all—has it black on white from one of his colleagues, and the Bishop can read the fearful challenge in our Discipline and ordain the man an elder in the Church of God !

What is the inference? That Bishop Dubs knowingly ordained a man an elder in the Church of God who was a slanderer and a liar, unless the Bishop was guilty of the crime alleged against him, and in addition guilty of falsehood. Does the reader still wonder why we have these troubles in the Church? The language of our lamented and honored Bro. Rev. W. F. Schneider involuntarily comes to mind: "We have now for a Bishop in our Church a man with a conscience like India rubber, elastic enough to stretch or to shrink as may best suit his purposes, and I now apprehend woe will come upon the Evangelical Association."

Immediately after his suspension Dubs published a circular in which he assailed the trial conference, attempted to cast odium upon the witnesses, made statements which were utterly untrue, and published evidence which was wholly false, especially that of his friend and co-conspirator, John Schneider. He then removed to Chicago, and edited a German weekly called the *Allgemeine Deutsche Zeitung*, in which week after week he assailed the Church and its officers in the most vehement and reprehensible language. In addition he went about from place to place in the West and in the East wherever he was tolerated, preaching at camp-meetings and elsewhere, notwithstanding his suspension from the ministry by a trial conference, the legality of which he could not call into question. And yet his friends eulogized him for submitting to his suspension!

CHAPTER IX.

The Attempt to Disorganize the Church.

Long previous to the trial of R. Dubs, when his wickedness was becoming more and more public, and every one was convinced that an investigation into the accusations against him was inevitable, his followers and "friends" threatened that should any ecclesiastical action be taken against him, they would also prefer charges against the two other bishops and suspend them from office. William Huelster had said before any charges were preferred that it was likely that by the time the Spring conferences would be held the Church would have no Bishops. Rev. G. W. Domer, formerly of the Pittsburgh Conference, a nephew of Rev. J. D. Domer, said to a brother, an honored layman of that conference, whose testimony is in the writer's possession, but whose name is not given to save him from persecution : " There is some talk of bringing Bishop Dubs to trial ; if they do so the Church will be without a Bishop ; for charges will then also be brought against Bishops Esher and Bowman, and they will be suspended. *It will only take three elders to do it.*" Evidence of the same kind could be multiplied until it would fill pages. It is a fact which cannot be successfully contradicted. The "charges" brought against Bishops Esher and Bowman were first in retaliation for the charges brought against Dubs, and secondly for the purpose of disorganizing the Church, hoping that in the confusion which might follow it would enable the followers of Dubs and the adherents of the *Evangelical* to snatch the reins of government, or at least force some kind of compromise which would result to their advantage. If the Bishops could be kept away from the Annual Conferences under their control, and from those in which they hoped to have the majority, they might after all succeed in their plans. At this time the division of the Church was fully decided upon, unless in some way they might secure a majority. Dubs himself so declared to a minister of the New York Conference adding that " they would not go empty-handed either. They would take at least four churches in Chicago and one in Buffalo." (It seems Mr. Kaechele could not fulfill his part of the contract). Dubs also made the same statement to a friend in Cleveland, O. Having decided upon a division of the Church the bishops must first be set aside, as they very well knew that with either Bishop Esher or Bishop Bowman in the chair *a resolution to call a separate " General Conference " would not be voted upon, and no delegates elected to such a body.* In order to carry out their plan, it was an absolute necessity to " suspend " the bishops, and then keep them out of the chair of the conference by " brute force." Hence the proceedings against Bishop Esher and the writer were not simply against us as individuals. These proceedings were a part of the conspiracy. The conspiracy could not have been put in practical operation without " suspending the bishops." " *It only took three elders to do it.*" Whether there was any cause or not thus to " humiliate and disgrace " the bishops, and bring such a fearful reproach upon the Church, was not considered as of any consequence. The plan demanded it and hence it must be done.

It has been shown in this volume how long and how patiently we had borne with R. Dubs; how we had again and again called his attention in a kind and brotherly way to his faults; how, when this was of no avail, we exhorted him in more earnest terms; how we did our utmost to save him, even in a manner compromised ourselves to save him and his, but all to no purpose. There was no offense in all the long list of specifications setting forth his wrong-doing to which his colleagues had not personally called his attention, except perhaps his slanderous falsehood against Rev. M. Pfitzinger, and Mr.

E. B. Esher; but Bro. Pfitzinger in a truly Christian manner called Dubs' attention to the matter and requested him to correct it. Dubs never even condescended to answer Bro. M. Pfitzinger. How was it with him and his followers concerning Bishops Esher and Bowman? Did they ever, as Christian men should, call upon either and inquire about rumors affecting their moral or official character? Did either of the entire clique ever fulfill the requirements of the Discipline or the teaching of the Word of God in reference to our alleged faults? If we had gone wrong was it no part of their duty, as they still professed to be Christians and even Christian ministers, to attempt to convert us from the errors of our way, or at least call our attention to the alleged wrong? The writer ventures the assertion that there was not one among all the hosts of our accusers who was the possessor of sufficient manliness, much less enough of the spirit of Christ in them to act as the Bible and the Discipline directs. They did not even accord either a judicial hearing such as our Discipline directs before beginning proceedings. C. S. Haman, J. D. Woodring, and J. M. Rinker, had the courage to ask our senior Bishop to come eight hundred miles to see them in order to find out what they had against him! If these men were actually too ignorant to understand the plain provisions of our Discipline and go to to the Bishop if they have ought against him, they certainly as Christian ministers should have understood the plain teaching of the Word of God, and gone to the Bishop and informed him of what they considered wrong in his conduct. And so without any personal examination of the Bishop, such as our Discipline directs, and to which he was entitled by the common law of men as well as the law of God, they proceed to put this venerable servant of Christ under charges! Bishop Esher who had served the Church from his youth, had been a minister for more than forty years, and a Bishop for twenty and six years proclaimed to be under charges by C. S. Haman, and such striplings as J. D. Woodring and J. M. Rinker! The same is true of Anton Huelster, M. Stamm and W. H. Messner. They called at the writer's house, but they never made nor attempted to make an examination such as the Discipline directs. After they had been told that the writer had already been examined upon the same accusations and fully exonerated, they left his house as they told the writer for the purpose of holding a consultation as to how to proceed further, and never again returned to ask a single question about the rumors, etc.; nevertheless they placed him under "charges" and proceeded to call a "trial conference."

As the whole matter concerning these sham trials has been thoroughly inquired into by the General Conference it will be necessary to give here simply the findings and actions of that body without note or comment.

REPORT OF THE COMMITTEE OF FIFTEEN.

On Tuesday, October 6, Rev. R. Yeakel, being in the chair, the committee of fifteen, through its chairman, announced that the committee was ready to report on the affairs of the Bishops.

The Committee first reported on Bishop Esher's case as follows:

Your Committee, to whom was referred the matter of a certain examination of Bishop J. J. Esher held and had at Chicago, Ill., on December 14th, 1889, by Revs. J. Lerch, H. J. Kiekhoefer and S. L. Umbach, elders in the Evangelical Association, and of certain proceedings thereafter undertaken and prosecuted against the same bishop at Reading, Pa., during the months of January, February and March, 1890, by Revs. C. S. Haman, J. D. Woodring, J. M. Rinker and others, having fully inquired into the said matter, all parties concerned having had full opportunity to appear and be heard thereupon, respectfully report, as their findings and conclusions, as follows:

I.

As to the facts of and connected with, the said examination by Revs. Lerch, Kiekhoefer and Umbach

A. That immediately after the last General Conference in 1887, certain ministers of our Church, including some of the members of the said General Conference, notably such as belonged to the East Pa., Central Pa., Pittsburgh and Illinois Conferences, violently attacked the proceedings of said General Conference, especially such portions thereof as related to the deposition, by that Conference, of the editor of the *Evangelical Messenger* and to the election of the general officers of the Church, including the election of the members of the Board of Publication; that this adverse movement against the said General Conference culminated in the organization of a stock company a few weeks after the General Conference, at Harrisburg, Pa., in order the better to start an independent newspaper as the organ or mouth-piece of the ministers and movement alluded to; that as the editor-in-chief of the newspaper so established, there was elected the former editor of the *Evangelical Messenger* who, as hereinbefore mentioned, had been deposed by the General Conference of 1887 after due trial;

That in said newspaper, almost from its first issue, in December, 1887, the General Conference of 1887 was violently assailed; charges and accusations were indiscriminately made against the same and individual members thereof, including all of the general officers of the Church (excepting Bishop R. Dubs); that the attacks upon Bishop J. J. Esher were of special virulence, his official and private character being assailed with unusual severity and accusations made against him, very frequently in and by anonymous communications, that these attacks increased in intensity from week to week—Bishop Esher being charged with and accused of intrigue, falsehood, slander, creating dissension in the Church and other alleged offenses, all having reference, to a great extent, indeed wholly, to his official action in and relation to Church affairs and to his communications published in our Church organs;

That in addition to these charges and accusations, like and similar charges and rumors were circulated and spread by means of a printed pamphlet, purporting to be edited by Rev. W. F. Heil, of the East Pa. Conference, and were also spread privately by the supporters of said newspapers in many parts of our Church, especially in Pennsylvania, Illinois and other western parts of our Church;

That as the result of the unbridled circulation of the charges, accusations and rumors referred to, among our ministers and laity, they became and were of general knowledge, and caused great harm in our Church, and engendered a spirit of mistrust in Bishop Esher, one of our general superintendents and general representatives of our Church, as well as in other general officers; that Bishop Esher repeatedly, both in public and private, requested and earnestly urged his accusers to substantiate their charges and accusations against him, if they could, in the manner provided in our Discipline and according to the way pointed out by Holy Writ, but his requests and appeals were not only refused, but themselves became the object of ridicule and vituperation by the very men who were accusing him;

That on account of these almost limitless assaults upon Bishop Esher, the senior Bishop of our Church, who since 1863 had continuously been one of our general superintendents, affairs in certain portions of the Church were in the Summer and Fall of 1889 in a critical condition; confidence began to be shaken in the General Conference of 1887 itself, which Conference Bishop Esher had publicly and privately defended, only the more to be a target for renewed charges and accusations.

B. Your committee further finds, that prominent among the persons who assisted in and themselves circulated the charges, accusations and rumors against Bishop Esher were certain of the leading ministers of the Illinois Conference; that ministers and members residing in the bounds of that Conference were well aware of the accusations and rumors referred to and of their import; that in the Fall of 1889 prominent laymen of that Conference becoming alarmed at the state of affairs, met in Chicago and determined and did request all the Bishops of our Church to address a general meeting of laymen and inform them what really lay at the bottom of the agitation in the Church. Bishop Bowman acceded to this request personally, and Bishop Esher also complied by sending to the laymen, at their convention in the Fall of 1889, a letter, which was afterwards published in our Church organs in October, 1889, by order of the convention itself.

C. That thereafter, there being no change for the better, but the charges, accusations and rumors against Bishop Esher being renewed with increased vigor and intensity, three prominent and well known elders of our Church, in good standing, namely: Rev. J. Lerch, of the Illinois Conference, Rev. H. J. Kiekhoefer, of the Wisconsin Conference, and acting president of the North-Western College at Naperville, Ill., and the Rev. S. L. Umbach, of the Canada Conference, and senior Professor in the Union Biblical Institute, also at Naperville, being, as the proofs before your committee show, well aware of the charges, accusations and rumors made and circulated against Bishop Esher (including those of slander, falsehood, creating dissension in the Church by reviving old matters, etc.), determined it to be their duty, as elders in the Church, to examine the Bishop concerning the same in accordance with the provisions of the Discipline of our Church; that their attention was also directed to said matters, and a thorough examination of the Bishop urged by an officer of the Illinois Conference Laymen's Association, in his representative capacity and thereto especially authorized, who also especially drew the attention of the said three elders to the contents of the letter hereinbefore referred to, which Bishop Esher had by request written to the laymen and had been read at their convention in Chicago in the Fall of 1889, and which letter Bishop Esher's accusers used as a pretext for renewed violent attacks on him, especially through and by the Harrisburg newspapers and its supporters.

D. That thereafter, namely on the 14th day of December,

1889, the said three elders went to Chicago, where Bishop Esher resided, met him, and, as the evidence before your committee establishes, in good faith examined him in accordance with our Discipline upon and concerning all the said accusations and rumors theretofore made and circulated against him, both those which related to each and all of his communications, which appeared in the official organs of the Church since the General Conference of 1887, including a certain communication addressed " To the Ministers and Members of the Evangelical Association," dated December 11, 1888, and which appeared in the *Evangelical Messenger*, a communication addressed to the chairman and members of the laymen convention, dated September 16, 1889, and published in the Church organs in October, 1889, as well as a communication entitled "That Confession," dated September 27, 1889, and published in our Church organs, and an article headed " North-Western College," also published in the *Evangelical Messenger*, June 25, 1889, as well as others.

That after a full and thorough examination of the Bishop upon all these matters and due investigation thereof, the three elders withdrew and afterwards, after due deliberation, were of the opinion and found that all of said charges and rumors were wholly unfounded and unjust, and decided that there was no cause for further proceedings against the bishop concerning said matters ; that on December 21, 1889, they informed Bishop Esher by letter concerning their findings.

That in the issues of the *Christliche Botschafter* and *Evangelical Messenger*, our official organs of February 17 and 18, 1890, respectively, the said three elders inserted an official notification, duly informing the Church of their said examination and concerning their findings and conclusions thereunder.

CONCLUSION OF SAID EXAMINATION HELD BY REVS. LERCH, KIEKHOEFER AND UMBACH.

Your Committee, being fully advised of and concerning all the facts of said examination and acquittal of Bishop Esher does, after due deliberation, find and report as its conclusions thereon and of said findings, as follows :

First, That said examination was held and had in strict accord with the letter and spirit of our Church Discipline, laws and institutions.

Second, That said examination was held and had and the findings thereunder were reached in absolute good faith without collusion whatsoever, either on the part of Bishop Esher, or any of his friends, and the said three elders or any of them.

Third, That said three elders, for the purpose of making such examination had, under the Discipline of the Evangelical Association, full jurisdiction of the subject matter and person, and that their findings constituted and were an acquittal of Bishop Esher of the said accusations and rumors, and were a final and conclusive adjudication of the subject matter.

Fourth, That the said findings of the three elders, Lerch, Kiekhoefer and Umbach, were binding on Bishop Esher and every minister and member of our Church, and disqualified absolutely every minister and member of our Church, having notice thereof, thereafter to again cause Bishop Esher to be examined or put upon trial upon the same subject matter on which he had been examined and found innocent by said three elders, and absolutely disqualified any preacher of the Evangelical Association to try him on such matters or participate in any such trial, before the General Conference next following.

Fifth, That the findings of said three elders made it the duty of Bishop Esher not again to submit to any attempted second examination upon the same subject matter before the next General Conference. A Bishop of our Church when proceeded against in his official capacity has no right or power to waive anything of such a nature as will thereby affect the interests of the Church whose agent or servant he is ; Bishop Esher, having been examined and found innocent by the said three elders, in good faith and in accordance with the Discipline and institutions of the Evangelical Association, and the said three elders having in good faith found that there was no cause for further proceedings on the matter concerning which they examined him, could not thereafter have been lawfully proceeded against upon the same subject matter covered in such examination by the elders Lerch, Kiekhoefer and Umbach. To recognize the contrary would be a violation not only of our Discipline and laws, but of the teaching of Christ, the great Head of our Church.

Sixth, That the communications published in the *Christliche Botschafter* of February 17, 1890, and in the *Evangelical Messenger* of February 18, 1890, by the elders Lerch, Kiekhoefer and Umbach, was an official and valid notice of their said examination and findings to the entire Church, and that every minister and member of our Church was bound to take notice thereof, without any further affirmative action on the part of said three elders or any of them or of Bishop Esher; that in case thereafter any person considered it necessary that the charges and accusations and rumors, or any of them, made and circulated against Bishop Esher concerning his conduct prior to December 14, 1889, be investigated or he be examined thereon, or any three elders considered an examination of the Bishop necessary concerning them, it would have been and was his or their duty, in any event, in honesty and good faith, to first have ascertained from elders Lerch, Kiekhoefer and Umbach, or either of them, as to whether their examination included the same subject matter covered by the charges, accusations or rumors on which such subsequent examination was contemplated; and if informed in the affirmative, such persons had no further jurisdiction of the same or of the Bishop and were disqualified further to act or proceed thereon.

Seventh, That after a full inquiry into the merits of the subject matter on which Bishop Esher was examined by said three elders, made by this committee as directed by this General Conference on the special request of Bishop Esher and said three elders, and being fully advised concerning the same, your committee finds that the conclusions and findings reached by said three elders, namely, that Bishop Esher was wholly innocent, and that there was no cause for further proceedings, were justified and fully warranted by the facts.

II.

As to the proceedings instituted and had against Bishop Esher, in January February and March, 1890, at Reading, Pa., and after his examination and acquittal by the elders Lerch, Kiekhoefer and Umbach, in December, 1880, your Committee having heard testimony concerning the same and being fully advised thereon, finds and reports as follows:

" A." That about January 9, 1890, and after formal charges had been lodged against Bishop Dubs, four preachers and members of the East Pa. Conference, viz., Revs, A. M. Stirk, S. S. Chubb, B. J. Smoyer and W. F. Heil, delivered to three other preachers and members of the same conference, viz., Revs. C. S. Haman, J. M. Rinker and J. Woodring, a document by them signed containing charges against Bishop Esher;

That said Haman, Rinker and Woodring accepted said document and thereafter summoned Bishop Esher to come to Reading, Pa., and "meet them, so that they might be able to perform their disciplinary duty," viz., " examine him ; "

That about one month after they had formally accepted the document referred to, Haman, Rinker and Woodring, on or about February 7th, caused a copy thereof to be delivered to Bishop Esher at his home in Chicago through Rev. John Schneider;

That prior to February 7th, Bishop Esher was ignorant of the contents of the document referred to, a copy of which is hereto attached for the information of this General Conference, marked " Paper 1; "

That on informing himself of the contents of the copy so delivered to him on February 7th, Bishop Esher, as soon as practicable, viz., on Monday, February 10th, 1890, returned the same to Haman, Woodring and Rinker, and at the same time informed them that he had already been examined before he had received their first letter, which was dated January 17th, 1890;

That on February 18, 1890, said Haman, Woodring and Rinker met at Reading, Pa., and, assuming to act in the capacity of three examining elders, without any evidence before them and in the absence of Bishop Esher, undertook to pass upon the document referred to, and did thereafter select, or aid in their selection, 17 preachers and convened them at Reading, Pa., on March 18, 1890, for the avowed purpose of trying Bishop Esher upon the matters and things against him contained in said document;

That the 17 persons so selected, and who convened at Reading, Pa., on March 18, 1890, did assume to constitute themselves into a trial conference to try Bishop Esher, upon the matters contained in said document, and on March 21st, still assuming to be a trial conference, passed a resolution declaring Bishop Esher suspended from his office as bishop and preacher until the next General Conference;

That Bishop Esher declined to submit to any and all of the said proceedings and ignored the pretended sentence of suspension;

"B." Your committee upon full inquiry finds the fact to be, that the said Revs. A. M. Stirk, S. S. Chubb, B. J. Smoyer, W. F. Heil, who signed said document, Revs. C. S. Haman, J. D. Woodring and J. M. Rinker, who assumed to act in the capacity of examining elders, had full knowledge and information on and prior to February 18, 1890, that the examination of Bishop Esher, at the hands of Revs. Lerch, Kiekhoefer and Umbach on December 14, 1889, covered and included all the subject matter of the charges and specifications contained in the document signed by said Stirk, Chubb, Smoyer and Heil, hereinbefore referred to, and that said elders, Lerch, Kiekhoefer and Umbach, in the capacity of three examining elders, had found Bishop

Esher guiltless thereof, and found there was no cause for further proceedings ;

That each and all of the 17 preachers, who met at Reading, Pa., on March 18, 1890, and on the 21st of the month, assumed to suspend Bishop Esher, then had, and did prior thereto have, full knowledge and information of and concerning said examination of Bishop Esher on December 14, 1889, and of his acquittal, that said examination included and covered all the subject matter contained in the document upon which they assumed to try Bishop Esher and suspend him.

CONCLUSIONS AS TO THE READING PROCEEDINGS.

Your committee is of the opinion and so reports, that, because and on account of the examination of Bishop Esher, by Revs. Lerch, Kiekhoefer and Umbach at Chicago, on Dec. 14, 1889, and of their findings by them, made as hereinbefore set forth, it was the duty of said Stirk, Smoyer, Chubb and Heil, as ministers of the Evangelical Association, to have withdrawn the charges, etc., by them signed, and abandoned further proceedings thereon, prior to March 19, 1890 ; that they were, prior to the said 19th of March, without authority to continue or aid in continuing proceedings thereon ;

That said Haman, Woodring and Rinker, having had notice of the prior examinations and findings of elders Lerch, Kiekhoefer and Umbach, had no jurisdiction whatever of the subject-matter contained in the document signed by Stirk, Chubb, Smoyer and Heil, or of the person of Bishop Esher, and were absolutely disqualified to proceed thereon, and that their pretended action in and concerning the same was wholly illegal, null and void ;

That the 17 persons met at Reading, Pa., on March 19, 1890, and held a pretended trial of Bishop Esher, had no jurisdiction whatsoever, either of the person of Bishop Esher or of the subject-matter on and concerning which they pretended to try the Bishop, and their proceedings, or pretended proceedings, were, one and all, wholly undisciplinary and their pretended findings and sentence were illegal, void and of no effect whatever under the Discipline and institutions of the Evangelical Association, either as to Bishop Esher or on the Church, or on any member thereof.

That the action of Bishop Esher in declining to submit to a second examination upon the same subject matter, on which he had theretofore examined and acquitted, was right and proper. To have done contrary would have been a betrayal of his high office and of the Church whose servant and representative he was. Even had he submitted to the pretended subsequent proceedings at Reading, the same would have been null and void and of no effect on the Church.

III.

Your Committee, in its inquiry into the said proceedings had against Bishop Esher, at Reading, Pa., and which, because of the prior examination and acquittal of the bishop, as herein before set forth, were wholly illegal, null and void, found that said proceedings at Reading, even had Bishop Esher not been theretofore examined and acquitted, were of such a nature as to have rendered them absolutely void under our Discipline and institutions. For instance:

First. It appears from the proofs before your committee, that Revs. Haman, Rinker and Woodring never contemplated going to the Bishop to examine him, but summoned him to go to them at Reading, Pa., 800 miles distant from Chicago, Bishop Esher's place of residence.

Your Committee is of the opinion that if three elders undertake to examine a bishop of our Church, it is their duty, under the Discipline, to go in a body to the bishop and examine him, or ot least *in good faith* to attempt to do so, and not to summon the Bishop, as did the Reading elders, to come to them. Failing to go to the Bishop at his place of residence, and in good faith making an attempt, at least, to examine the bishop there, is such a serious and fatal omission of disciplinary requirement, as will render void any further proceedings of such three elders in the matter.

Secondly. It further appears that on February 18, 1890, the said Haman, Woodring and Rinker, assuming, in the absence of Bishop Esher, and without any evidence before them, to pass upon the matter in the capacity of three examining elders, were not actually of the opinion, that Bishop Esher was guilty, and never informed the Bishop that they were of such an opinion.

Your Committee finds that it is the law of our Church that before three elders can, under our Discipline, proceed to place a bishop of our Church on trial before a trial conference, they must be actually of the opinion that the accused bishop is guilty, and under our institutions and laws, they must inform the bishop of that fact in plain terms, and not leave it to a mere possible inference; that this is a necessary prerequisite and a condition precedent to putting a bishop on trial. The fact that the Reading elders were not of such an opinion, but expressly and in writing stated another reason, why the bishop ought to be tried, rendered all their subsequent proceedings absolutely null and void.

Having seen fit to put their findings in writing, the three elders were bound thereby. The written report of their findings, made to the 17 persons they had convened at Reading on March 19, 1890, viz., "That the said charges against Bishop J. J. Esher are of so grave and serious a character and sufficiently well founded to require a thorough investigation," would have been wholly insufficient to confer jurisdiction on such 17 persons to try the Bishop. Convened under such circumstances the said persons, meeting at Reading on March 19–21, were absolutely without jurisdiction either of the subject-matter or of the person of Bishop Esher, and their pretended findings were a nullity.

Third. It further appears that Revs. Haman, Woodring and

Rinker never notified Bishop Esher where his trial was to be held, as by our Discipline and laws required.

This of itself, even if said persons would have had jurisdiction and would have been otherwise qualified, was such a fatal omission of a necessary prerequisite, as to have rendered all their subsequent proceedings under the laws and institutions of our Church absolutely void and of no effect.

Fourth. Your Committee, in its inquiry into the matter connected with the said Reading proceedings, ascertained the fact to be by overwhelming proof, that said proceedings from their formal inception in January, 1890, and to their close in March following, were but retaliatory and revengeful in their character and purpose on the part of all the persons therein participating; that prior to March 18, 1890, all of the 17 persons selected to try the Bishop, had, without exception, expressed themselves by formal vote as intensely hostile to the Bishop, and several had even declared that since proceedings had been begun against Bishop Dubs, now Bishops Esher and Bowman would and must be suspended also; that as early as February 5, 1890, being nearly two weeks before Haman, Woodring and Rinker had ever pretended to decide that a trial of Bishop Esher was necessary, the newspaper published at Harrisburg, herein before referred to, was able to inform its readers that Bishop Esher would be tried in the East and Bishop Bowman in the West; and in this connection the Committee also specially begs to refer to the utterly illegal course in attempting to try a member of our Church at a place distant 800 miles from his place of residence. Such a course, we are free to say, has never before been taken in the history of our Church.

Your Committee cannot, in the limited time accorded it, embody in this their report the evidence at length before it of the gross fraud at the Reading proceedings. It is convinced of the appalling fact that ministers of our Church did deliberately conspire together at Reading, Pa., in the early part of 1890, indeed previously thereto, to manufacture charges and accusations against Bishop Esher, then scheme how best to convict him thereon and having fully, as they supposed, accomplished their purpose, made it the pretext of publishing to the world a pamphlet purporting to contain a full account of "The trial and conviction of Bishop J. J. Esher." Your Committee is convinced that this was done primarily to ruin the official and private character of Bishop Esher.

Your Committee begs to report that proceedings instituted and consummated against a bishop, minister or member of our Church under such circumstances as characterized the said proceedings against Bishop Esher, are not only absolutely null and void under the Discipline of our Church, but deserve to be stamped as maliciously wicked and treated accordingly. Not only do the Discipline and laws of our Church forbid such proceedings, but they are in direct violation of the Word of God, upon which our Church is founded.

SUMMARY.

Your Committee finds and reports, that the proceedings instituted and had against Bishop Esher at Reading, Pa., and which culminated on March 21, 1890, in his alleged suspension, were absolutely null and void, and as though they had never been had at all, and in no way, shape or manner affected Bishop J. J. Esher, either as bishop or minister of our Church.

The following was then unanimously adopted by a rising vote:

The General Conference having heard the report of the special committee of 15, to whom was referred the matter of a certain examination, and acquittal of Bishop J. J. Esher, in the month of December, 1889, at Chicago Ill., and to whom were also referred for inquiry certain other subsequent proceedings had against said Bishop at Reading, Pa., in January February and March, 1890, wherein certain preachers undertook to try and suspend him from his office of bishop and minister, and this body now having fully considered the grounds of said report, and being duly advised thereon; be it

Resolved, That said report be and hereby is, in all respects adopted, approved and confirmed.

Whereupon the Conference with deep emotion joined in singing the doxology, in both the German and English languages.

Then the venerable bishop with his faithful companion arose, and with deep feeling he thanked the Conference for the protection which she granted him and his family, and declared their willingness to serve God faithfully unto the end, as they had endeavored to do to the present hour.

The Committee next reported on the affair of Bishop Thomas Bowman.

REPORT OF THE COMMITTEE OF FIFTEEN IN THE MATTER OF BISHOP THOMAS BOWMAN.

In the matter of a certain examination of Bishop Thomas Bowman, held and had by three elders of our Church, viz., Rev. Jesse Lerch, Rev. J. H. Kiekhoefer, and Rev. S. L. Umbach, on December 19, 1889, and of certain proceedings thereafter instituted and carried out against the same bishop in the months of January, February and March, 1890, at Chicago, Ill., by Revs. H. Messner, M. Stamm, Anton Huelster and others, your Committee, to whom said matter was referred by the General Conference, after full inquiry thereof, all parties concerned having had full opportunity to be heard thereon, respectfully present as their report on their findings and conclusions the following:

I.

Of and concerning the facts of the examination of Bishop Bowman by the elders, Lerch, Kiekhoefer and Umbach.

"A." That for several years prior to the General Conference of 1887 there existed a movemnet in our Church that had for its object the attainment of all the general offices of our Church for the adherents of said movement, which was headed by Bishop R. Dubs, H. B. Hartzler and others; that the better to attain the end in view, the chief actors in said movement began a systematic attack on Bishops Bowman, Esher, the Board of Missions, Board of Publication, and on other officers of our Church, in the columns of the *Evangelical Messenger*, our English church organ, then edited by Rev. H. B. Hartzler.

That at the General Conference of 1887, the said Hartzler was deposed from his office, as editor after due trial, and the objects had in view by the participants of said movement with but one exception totally miscarried.

That on this account some of the delegates to the General Conference repudiated its proceedings, especially those parts relating to the election of general church officials and to the conviction and deposition of said Hartzler, and did organize an independent newspaper at Harrisburg, Pa., electing as its editor-in-chief, said H. B. Hartzler, and made arrangements for a campaign of attacks, upon the said General Conference and the general officials (excepting Bishop Dubs), elected in 1887.

That not only through the columns of said newspaper, but by word of mouth, and by means of a printed pamphlet, of which Rev. W. F. Heil was the reputed author, the General Conference was energetically attacked and Bishop Bowman assaulted, both as to his official and moral character. These assaults on Bishop Bowman became more fierce as time progressed, and many accusations were openly made against him. Almost every article or communication published by him in our Church organs and his utterances in general were indiscriminately assailed and serious accusations against him made concerning them. These accusations among others included those of falsehood, slander and intrigue. During the Summer and Fall of 1889 the accusations and rumors affecting the Bishop's moral character were of general knowledge throughout the Church, especially in the bounds of the Illinois Conference, some of whose members were and had been for months assiduously circulating the same privately and publicly.

So serious was the condition of affairs, occasioned by these attacks on Bishop Bowman and other general officers of our Church, that leading laymen of the Illinois Conference, alarmed at matters in this conference and in the Church generally, held formal meetings and conventions in the Fall and early Winter of 1889, for the purpose, if possible, to stop the agitation in the Church, well knowing that the accusations and rumors against Bishop Bowman were one of the main causes of such agitation, and it being apparent that Bishop Bowman's accusers purposely refrained from causing the Bishop to be examined thereon and thus dispose of the matter in a disciplinary manner, one of the general officers of the laymen's organization in Illinois did, in his representative capacity, specially call to the attention of Reverends J. Lerch, H. J. Kiekhoefer, of the Wisconsin Conference and acting President of North-Western College, and S. L. Umbach, Professor of Theology in the Union Biblical Institute (said institutions being located at Naperville, Ill., a suburb of Chicago), the fact that Bishop Bowman was accused of serious offenses, and that an examination ought to be made ;

That said three ministers were elders in good standing in our Church, prominent and well known, and were, and for a long time had been, well aware of the accusations and rumors made and circulated against Bishop Bowman.

Considering it to be their duty as elders in the Church to examine the Bishop on and concerning said accusations and rumors, the said three elders did on the 19th day of December, 1889, at Naperville, Ill., meet the Bishop and in accordance with our Discipline examined him on and concerning all such rumors and accusations, and on the completion of their said examination, they withdrew and thereafter, viz., on December 23, 1889, after due deliberation came to the conclusion and found that the accusations and rumors so made and circulated about the Bishop were without foundation in fact, and that there was no cause for further proceedings against the Bishop;

That they duly informed Bishop Bowman of their proceedings in writing dated December 23rd, 1889, and afterwards caused to be inserted an official notification concerning their said examination and findings in the *Christliche Botschafter*, dated February 17, and *Evangelical Messenger*, February 18, 1890, respectively;

That said examination was held and conducted and the findings reached in absolute good faith and without collusion on the part of any person or persons concerned.

CONCLUSIONS AS TO SAID EXAMINATION.

Your Committee being fully advised of all the facts concerning said examination and after due deliberation finds and reports as its conclusions thereon and on said findings as follows:

1. That said examination so conducted in good faith, was held strictly in accordance with our Discipline and as thereby and the institutions of our Church contemplated;

2. That said elders, Lerch, Kiekhoefer and Umbach, in their said examination had under the Discipline of the Evangelical Association full jurisdiction of the subject-matter and of the person of Bishop Bowman, and their findings therein constituted and were an acquittal of Bishop Bowman and were a final and conclusive adjudication of the subject-matter;

3. That the said findings of the said three elders were binding on Bishop Bowman and on every minister and member of our Church, and disqualified absolutely every such minister and member, having notice thereof, thereafter again to cause Bishop Bowman to be examined, or put upon trial upon the same subject-matter on which he had been examined and acquitted by said three elders and disqualified any preacher of the Evangelical Association thereafter to try the Bishop on the same subject-matter, or participate in any such trial;

4. That the findings of said three elders precluded Bishop Bowman from lawfully submitting to a second examination on the same subject-matter. Having been once examined and acquitted in good faith and in accordance with our Discipline, as the proofs show he had been, he could not thereafter have been lawfully proceeded against on the same subject-matter. The Discipline and institutions of the Evangelical Association, if construed in the light of the teachings of Christ, as we are in duty bound to construe them, do not and never did contemplate that either so high an officer as bishop or the humblest member could lawfully be re-examined upon the same subject matter on which he had once in good faith been examined and found innocent. The provisions of our Discipline regarding alleged transgressing members, ministers and bishops are not punitive, but reformatory in their object ;

5. That the communications published in our Church organs on February 17, and February 18, 1890, by the elders J. Lerch, H. J. Kiekhoefer and S. L. Umbach, giving notice of their examination of Bishop Bowman and their findings, was an official and valid notice thereof to the entire Church, and of itself bound every minister and member therein to take notice of such examinations and findings, without any further and other affirmative action, either on the part of said three elders or of Bishop Bowman ;

6. That, as instructed by the General Conference, on request of Bishop Bowman and said three examining elders, your Committee made a full inquiry into the merits of the subject-matter on which Bishop Bowman was examined by said three elders, and being fully advised concerning the same, your Committee finds that the conclusions and findings reached by said three elders, viz., that Bishop Bowman was innocent of the said accusations and rumors, and no cause existed for further proceedings, were fully warranted by the facts, and that justice and right demanded the same.

II.

As the proceedings instituted and had against Bishop Bowman in January, February and March, 1890, being after his examination and acquittal by elders Lerch, Kiekhoefer and Umbach, your Committee, having heard testimony and being duly advised concerning the same, finds as follows :

"A." That on or about January 28th, 1890, being some time after charges had been lodged against Bishop Dubs, a document containing charges, etc., against Bishop Bowman, signed by W. F. Heil, Wm. Caton and H. Meier, was placed into the hands of Reverends H. Messner, Anton Huelster and M. Stamm. and by them formally accepted, a copy of which document, marked "Paper 2," accompanies this report for the better information of the General Conference ;

That six days before said Messner, Stamm and Huelster had received said document, said A. Huelster had by letter arranged with Bishop Bowman for a meeting on January 28th, being the day said document was delivered to them, for the purpose of holding an examination of the Bishop ;

That on the afternoon of January 28, 1890, the said three persons, being elders and members of the Illinois Conference, went in a body and met Bishop Bowman at his place of residence in Chicago, when and where they informed the Bishop that said document had been placed in their hands, and that they had come in the capacity of three examining elders ;

That they then proceeded to read the said document to the Bishop, who, after he had thus been informed and had knowledge as to its contents, informed them, then and there, that he had already been examined on all the subject-matter in said document contained, by elders Lerch, Kiekhoefer and Umbach, and thereon acquitted ;

That thereafter said Messner, Stamm and Huelster undertook to call together fifteen ministers to try Bishop Bowman on the matters and things contained in said document, and fixed the date for such trial on March 5, 1890, at Chicago, when and where such alleged trial was held, and the persons thus meeting assumed to suspend Bishop Bowman from his office as bishop and preacher of the Evangelical Association.

Your Committee on due inquiry finds the fact to be, that on and prior to March 5, 1890, all of the parties connected with the proceedings, taken and had against Bishop Bowman upon said document, had due notice and knowledge of the prior examination of Bishop Bowman by elders Lerch, Kiekhoefer and Umbach, and of their findings thereon, and that the subject-matter of all the charges and specifications contained in said document, signed by Reverends Heil, Caton and Meier, and upon which said persons assumed to try and suspend Bishop Bowman in March, 1890, at Chicago, had been covered and included in said prior examination of the Bishop by the elders Lerch, Kiekhoefer and Umbach, and the Bishop found innocent thereof;

"B." That the said persons so connected with the said subsequent proceedings against Bishop Bowman and participating therein, although having due information of such prior examination and acquittal, did, notwithstanding, totally ignore the same and continue said proceedings as above mentioned.

CONCLUSIONS AS TO THE CHICAGO PROCEEDINGS.

Your Committee is of the opinion, and so reports, that on and prior to March 5, 1890, it was the duty of said Heil, Caton and Meier, as ministers and members of the Evangelical Association, to have withdrawn their said charges, etc., against Bishop Bowman, and abandoned further proceedings thereon;

That said Messner, Stamm and Huelster had no authority under the Discipline of the Evangelical Association to call a meeting of ministers to try Bishop Bowman upon the matters and things in said document, so signed by Heil, Caton and Meier, contained, that they were without jurisdiction of the same or of the person of Bishop Bowman, and all their doings and proceedings concerning the matter, including the convening by them of an alleged conference at Chicago on March 5, 1890, were illegal and of no effect whatever;

That the said fifteen persons who met at Chicago on March 5, 1890, to try Bishop Bowman, had no jurisdiction whatever over the subject-matter or of Bishop Bowman, and their proceedings, one and all, were wholly undisciplinary and their pretended findings illegal, null and void, and without any effect either on Bishop Bowman or the Church, or any minister or member therein;

That Bishop Bowman, in refusing to submit to a second examination on the same subject-matter upon which he had once been examined and acquitted, performed but his duty to the Church. Had he taken a different course in said matter, he would have betrayed the high trust reposed in him by our Discipline as bishop. A bishop of the Evangelical Association can not lawfully ignore the findings of a disciplinary body, such as elders Lerch, Kiekhoefer and Umbach did in fact constitute, if such findings are reached in good faith and with an honest purpose, as was the case in the said examination and findings by said three elders last above named.

Your Committee therefore finds that the proceedings instituted and had against Bishop Bowman, based upon the document signed by Wm. Caton, W. F. Heil and H. Meier, and formally accepted by H. Messner, M. Stamm and A. Huelster on January 28, 1890, and upon which certain fifteen persons at Chicago, at a meeting held beginning March 5, 1890, assumed to suspend Bishop Bowman, were under the Discipline, laws and institutions of the Evangelical Association wholly illegal, null and void.

III.

Your Committee in its inquiry into said proceedings had against Bishop Bowman, of Chicago, Ill., and which your Committee finds were wholly illegal, null and void, because of the prior examination of the Bishop and the findings thereupon had, ascertained and found that said Chicago proceedings, even had there been no such prior trial, examination and acquittal, were of such a nature as to render them absolutely void under our Discipline and institutions, for instance :

1. It was clearly established by the proofs that Reverends Messner, Stamm and Huelster, on the occasion of their meeting Bishop Bowman on January 28th, 1890, after being informed by the Bishop that he had already been examined and acquitted by elders Lerch, Kiekhoefer and Umbach, withdrew for the avowed purpose of consulting together as to the effect of such prior examination, without making an effort even to examine the Bishop concerning the charges, etc., in their possession, and that they did not thereafter return or even pretend to make such an examination.

Your Committee is of the opinion that as the Discipline of our Church in plain language makes an examination of a bishop and an actual opinion of guilt a condition precedent to putting him on trial, the action of said Messner, Stamm and Huelster in calling together an alleged trial conference to try Bishop Bowman was wholly unauthorized and illegal ;

That, failing to make an examination at all, or in good faith attempting so to do (which omission the said Messner, Stamm and Huelster were guilty of), said three persons could not honestly and in good faith and as by our Discipline contemplated have been of opinion, and they were not actually of opinion, that Bishop Bowman was guilty of any crime as by our Discipline they would have been required to be before they could lawfully proceed further.

2. It further appeared to your Committee that the fifteen persons assuming to try and suspend Bishop Bowman did not in fact convict or pretend to convict him on the charges or pretended charges upon which they assumed to try the Bishop.

Their findings were as follows :

" 1." That specifications 1 and 10, under charge 2nd, are not sufficiently sustained by direct testimony ;

"2." That all other specifications under charges 1, 2 and 3 are sufficiently sustained by the testimony presented to this conference, to convict the Bishop of conduct unbecoming a minister and bishop of the Evangelical Association;

"3." That, therefore, in accordance with direction of our Discipline, Bishop Thomas Bowman be suspended from office as bishop and preacher of the Evangelical Association, until the session of General Conference in 1891.

Such findings were not responsive to the charges and consequently void, of no effect, and wholly insufficient to authorize a trial conference to lawfully suspend a bishop from our Church, and an alleged suspension of a bishop based upon such a finding has absolutely no effect whatever and is void.

3. Your Committee in its investigation into the matter to it referred found the fact to be, that the proceedings instituted and had against Bishop Bowman at Chicago were the result of a deliberately laid scheme to convict him at all hazards because of the prior suspension of Bishop R. Dubs.

The persons connected with the proceedings against Bishop Bowman were staunch supporters of the newspaper at Harrisburg hereinbefore alluded to, by and through which the charges and accusations against the Bishop had been chiefly circulated, and the men who were the chief actors in said proceedings had been prominently engaged in spreading and circulating the very matters upon which they themselves afterward assumed to try the Bishop. It was established by the proofs that two of the three elders who assumed to act in the capacity of examining elders, viz., Messner and Stamm, and who above all others should have been unprejudiced, themselves appeared before the trial committee, whom they had selected, as leading witnesses, and gave testimony against the Bishop on the merits of the case; that all three of the said elders, Messner, Stamm and Huelster, had only a few hours before they went to the Bishop on January 28, 1890, held a meeting with certain parties who were then and had been for two years in rebellion against our General Conference, and of whom some thereafter acted as jurors and appeared as witnesses at the Chicago trial. Your Committee is convinced that Messner, Stamm and A. Huelster were but the willing tools in the hands of more prominent ministers who had determined upon suspending the Bishop. The whole proceedings were, as the testimony proves, redolent with fraud, and hence not only totally void, but under our Discipline and the Word of God a crime against the Bishop and the Evangelical Association.

SUMMARY.

Your Committee finds and reports, that the proceedings instituted and had against Bishop Bowman in Chicago in January, February and March, 1890, and his alleged suspension were absolutely null and void, and that he was not thereby affected, either as bishop or as a minister of the Evangelical Association.

The above report having been presented, the following was unanimously adopted by a rising vote:

The General Conference having heard the report of the Special Committee of 15, to whom was referred the matter of a certain examination and acquittal of Bishop Thos. Bowman, in the month of December 1889, at Naperville, Ill., and to whom were also referred for inquiry certain other subsequent proceedings had against the said Bishop at Chicago, Ill., in January, February and March, 1890, wherein certain preachers undertook to try and suspend him from his office of bishop and minister, and this body now having fully considered the grounds of said report and being duly advised thereon; be it

Resolved, That said report be and hereby is in all respects adopted, approved and confirmed.

CHAPTER X.

Attempts to Alienate Church Property in the Interests of the Rebellion.

NORTH-WESTERN COLLEGE.

Originally North-Western College was brought into existence through the united efforts of four Annual Conferences, the Illinois, the Wisconsin, the Indiana and the Iowa, each being entitled to equal rights of possession and management. These Conferences, however, soon discovered that in order to put the College on a good financial basis in securing the accumulation of a sufficient endowment and a respectable number of students, it was necessary to invite other Annual Conferences to unite with them. Hence the Board of Trustees made arrangements to this end, and for this purpose authorized their agents to visit other Annual Conferences and prevail on them to unite in the compact. In due time the New York, the Canada, the Michigan, the Ohio, the South Indiana, the Des Moines and Kansas Conferences accepted the propositions made to them and entered the union. The condition offered these conferences was that they should have equal rights with the four original conferences in ownership and management, each Annual Conference being entitled to a representative in the Trustee Board, the territory of such conference to be open for the collection of funds for the college by an agent as the Trustees might direct. In addition the conferences obligated themselves to take up an annual educational collection for the benefit of the college. Not only was this offer made, but it was strongly urged by the different agents, John Schneider, Samuel Dickover and William Huelster, and it was considered quite a success whenever the agent or treasurer succeeded in inducing an additional conference to join the compact. Usually the presiding Bishop united with the agent in accomplishing such a result, feeling this to be in the interest of higher education in our Church. Bishop Esher having been connected with the college from its commencement, having been its first agent, and feeling an especial interest in its welfare, did all he could to have the conferences unite. The offers were made and accepted in good faith. All the conferences, with possibly one or two exceptions, have also been canvassed in the interests of the college, and paid liberally towards the endowment fund.

Finding this plan of enlarging the constituency of the college working so favorably in every way, the trustees of the Union Biblical Institute agreed to adopt the same plan in its interests. Judge Cody, of Naperville, Ill., who had been the counsel for the college and institute corporations, was therefore instructed to draw up papers to have the charter of the U. B. Institute so changed that this might be done. In the course of this work Judge Cody discovered a law upon the statute books of the State requiring that two-thirds of the trustees of an educational institution located within the State of Illinois must be residents of the State. This discovery at once revealed the fact that the college plan which had been apopted and entered into on all sides in absolute good faith, was illegal. Here was a dilemna. All connected with the college at that time were agreed that an effort must be made at once to have this law amended or changed so that the agreement which had been made could be carried out, otherwise the college would suffer very materially, and the conferences which had accepted the proposition made by the Board of Trustees, through their agents, would be greatly wronged. *There was no dissenting voice on this question when the discovery was made by Judge Cody in reference to the laws of the State.* The Board of Trustees at its first session after this fact became known *unanimously* adopted a resolution that efforts should be made to have the law changed so that the contract and agreement which had been made could be carried out. While it was taken for granted that the trustees of the college, who first made the offer and induced the other Annual Conferences to accept their proposition, are acquainted with the laws of the State under which they were incorporated, the conferences in other States were not expected to be acquainted with the laws of Illinois, and had a right to believe the propositions and offers made them were legal—hence the honor of the board which originally made the offer, as well as of the individuals through whom the offers were made, was largely involved. In order to accomplish the desired end, the trustee board appointed a committee, of which President H. H. Rassweiler was chairman. A petition was drawn up and the matter was presented to the Illinois legislature and referred to the proper committee, and as the request seemed to be entirely reasonable, and the law as it stood so unreasonable, every one expected the desired amendment would pass at once without delay or opposition. However, there was a sudden hitch in the proceedings. The legislature adjourned without having had an opportunity to consider the bill.

In the meantime the "Illinois Conference Ring" had discovered its opportunity. It had long since desired to have full control of N. W. College and U. B. Institute. Had not their faithful ally and co-conspirator, R. Dubs, managed to be present at almost every session of the Trustee Board, although not in any wise officially connected with the same, as a kind of outside lobbyist to influence its action in favor of the "Illinois Ring?" Here the young people of a large portion of the Church were educated. Here many of the ministers were educated. It was therefore a matter of great importance, indeed of the greatest importance, to the Dubs party, to have complete control of these educational institutions. The dilemma furnished the opportunity. The "Illinois Ring" has a meeting and appoints one of its number, Rev. William Huelster, the very person, who went from one conference session to another, and pleaded in his clever manner until he prevailed upon the conferences to accept the proposition offered them, to go to Springfield, Ill., where the Legislature convenes, and smother the required legislation! President H. H. Rassweiler, instead of pushing the matter as he obligated himself to do by accepting the chairmanship of the Committee, if he did not use his influence at the behests of the "Illinois Ring" against the required legislation, certainly did nothing for it, and afterwards proposed to occupy a position of neutrality on this question if he should be continued as President. This speaks volumes under the circumstances. Was not his position previously even one of neutrality? In order that the reader may be fully informed upon this subject the action of the General Conference at Buffalo will be quoted:

"Inasmuch as a friendly letter addressed to the General Conference from Rev. J. Lerch, agent and treasurer of N. W. College and U. B. Institute, located at Naperville, Ill., was received by the committee, in which communication reference is made to the fact that the laws of said State do not harmonize with the charter of said college, inasmuch as the laws of said State require that an incorporated educational institution must have two-thirds of its trustees residents of that State, and since said provision conflicts with the present charter, and

"*Whereas*, Said institution belongs to our Church, recognized in the quadrennial messages of the bishops of our Church and inasmuch as General Conference is the Supreme Court of our Church, and we believe an expression from said body would give weight and influence to the Board of Trustees of said institutions and to the conferences connected with the same, therefore be it

"1. *Resolved*, That it is the sense of this committee with reference to the Annual Conferences connected with our institutions at Naperville, Ill., *that their rights as expressed in the original contract be recognized and must be kept inviolate in the future*, and that we recognize and approve the endeavors of the said trustees to have the laws of Illinois so amended as to render the charter legal and valid; and inasmuch as a petition was presented to the Illinois Legislature to have such an amendment passed, and since its passage both in the House of Representatives and of the Senate was looked upon with favor, *but was smothered by opposition*, therefore

"2. *Resolved*, That we deeply deplore the action of the opponents of said petition.

"3. *Resolved*, That we earnestly solicit the Board of Trustees to continue their efforts in urging such a petition until the desired amendment is secured."

The report of this committee was adopted without a dissenting vote. It would be too much to presume that the members of the "Illinois Ring" who were present at Buffalo voted for this report, and yet none of them voted against it. It would have been considered by them to be bad policy publicly to advocate and vote for a downright theft. But it was only a matter of policy for the time being until compelled to show their hands. The committee who formulated and presented the above report to the General Conference were, C. S. Haman, M. J. Carothers, H. E. Linse, C. F. Zimmerman, W. H. Bucks, C. Oertle, H. B. Hartzler, S. S. Chubb, J. Kaufman, E. Weiss, M. W. Steffey, M. L. Wing, D. B. Beyers, J. Walz, A. Holzwarth, and B. C. Oyler. S. C. Haman, formerly of the East Pa. Conference, chairman of the Committee, S. S. Chubb, also formerly of the same conference, M. J. Carothers, formerly a member of the Central Pa. Conference, aid in formulating this report and then afterwards join hands with the dishonest men who do their utmost to defeat the very directions they gave, and attempt to deprive the conferences of " their rights as expressed in the original contract." Even C. S. Haman now sits with them in "conference" and pretends to be their "Bishop." Should not a blush of shame tinge his face when he remembers the unholy alliance into which he has entered?

At a meeting of the Trustee Board of the College held in the Spring of 1888, the matter of securing the desired and urgently needed legislation came to a focus. The Board realized that the President of the College should not only be in full harmony with its efforts in this behalf, but that he must be ready under the circumstances, and in view of the opposition which had developed, to put forth strong and determined efforts in that direction. Hence the Board demanded of President Rassweiler that he should clearly define his position. After keeping the Board waiting for two days for an answer he finally replied that he would occupy a position of neutrality! This answer fully convinced the Board that the interests of the College under the circumstances demanded a change in the person of the President of that Institution, as the importance of securing the desired change in the laws of the State far outweighed every other interest of the College at that time. How the Board came to think of the writer to take this undesirable position, at this time and under these circumstances, is an unexplained mystery. He was in Minnesota at the time attending to his episcopal duties, not dreaming of such an occurrence. He had not been at all consulted about it and knew absolutely nothing about it until several days later. These are the facts notwithstanding all the misrepresentations which have been made.

At a later meeting of the board held in February, 1889, the President of the college was appointed by the board to visit Springfield, Ill., where the Legislature was in session, and advocate the passage of the bill drawn up by the attorneys of the board, Messrs. Judd, Ritchie & Esher, of Chicago. This bill had previously been presented to the House and Senate Committees on Education, and it had been agreed to hold special meetings of the committees to hear arguments from both sides. At this hearing by these honorable gentlemen, the opposition was represented by an attorney from Naperville, D. B. Byers and William Caton. Represented by D. B. Byers and William Caton! Both were delegates at the General Conference at Buffalo in 1887, when the report of the committee on education, instructing the Board of Trustees to secure the legislation in question, was adopted. D. B. Byers was even a member of that committee. Both pledged their honor as men and ministers to acquiesce in and obey the proceedings of that body. Both vowed at the holy altar to obey the "regulations of this

Association," and yet both of them appear as the mouthpieces of a wicked conspiracy in opposition to these regulations, in open violation of their solemn ordination vows, and of their pledged word and honor! Moreover, they oppose measures, and the only measures by which the "rights of the conferences as expressed in the original contract" could be secured, thus advocating not only the breaking of a solemn agreement, but the alienation of property valued at thousands of dollars from its owners. In full view of all these overt acts of rebellion against the Church these men only cry they are being persecuted when they are called "rebels." Is it a wonder that the persons who were compelled to meet these parties privately and publicly and defeat their plans and schemes were occasionally tempted to use language which, under other circumstances, might be considered "unbecoming?"

The hearing before the Committees of the Legislature presented a spectacle indeed. One of the Bishops of the Church, temporarily President of one of its colleges, in obedience to the instructions of the General Conference, and the Trustee Board of the institution, appearing before these committees of legislators to argue the necessity of a law of the State to save the institution and carry out a sacred contract; opposed by two ministers of the Church, both of whom it was shown had promised to obey their superiors in office, publicly opposing their own General Conference regulations, their own Bishop, and opposing the very measures by which alone a contract and agreement could only be carried out!

Probably the fight in the Legislature for the passage of the amendments was one of the most hotly contested battles in the legislative halls of the State at least for that year. The opposition had secured the aid of one of the most influential and ablest members of the Senate, which made the conflict all the more severe. Nevertheless when the final vote was reached, there was a decided majority in the Senate as well as in the House for our bill. Just before the final reading of the bill the

Illinois Conference met in session at Barrington, Ill., when the conspirators of that conference made one more desperate effort to defeat the bill by sending a telegram to be read in the Senate in which they set forth that it was un-American to have persons not residents of the State control educational institutions located in the State. Presumably the parties who signed their names to that telegram did not know that by the laws of the State of Illinois non-residents could build a furnace or a brewery, or commence any other business enterprise and fully control it and manage it as they saw fit;—only an educational institution, according to their ideas, must be an exception! In that view it would be American to build a Chinese wall around the State! However what made the telegram the more ridiculous was, that nearly all of the thirty-five names attached were German. Its only effect was to provoke laughter and make some votes for our bill.

These men not only publicly opposed the regulations of the General Conference, and thereby violated their ordination vows, but by this action attempted to deprive the Annual Conferences belonging to the college compact outside of Illinois of "their rights as expressed in the original contract," thus making themselves also guilty of dishonesty. Such men, among whom were A. Huelster, M. Stamm and H. Messner, of course could also institute proceedings against a Bishop of the Church to rob him of his rights and reputation, and disgrace and humiliate him before his Church and the world.

It is no more than just in this connection to recognize the services of the law firm engaged by the Board of Trustees to prevent the wholesale fraud contemplated by the conspirators in Illinois, namely Messrs. Judd, Ritchie and Esher. The principal labor, however, was done by Mr. E. B. Esher, who labored day and night for weeks until he grandly succeeded in gaining the desired object. The following resolution adopted by the Board of Trustees, after the battle was fought and won, may not be out of place:

"*Resolved,* That we especially thank Mr. E. B. Esher, as attorney and trustee of the college, for the dauntless energy which he showed in superintending and managing the college bill, and the fearlessness with which he grappled with the opposition, not only in defeating and breaking up their plans, but in pushing the contest on its merits, and ever holding before his friends and foes the true principles of justice and right, which won for him the victory, which has placed North-Western College in the hands of its owners."

The opposition, when the change of administration was made, failed not in prophesying the downfall of the college. They had succeeded in prejudicing and discouraging the citizens of Naperville to a large degree. Still all their prophecies however have failed. The college is doing exceedingly well. President Kiekhoefer has proved himself to be the right man in the right place. Since then a fine large additional building has been erected, the old building as well as the grounds also much improved. Steam heating and electric lighting has also been since introduced into both buildings.

John Schneider who represented the opposition element of the Illinois Conference, and William Huelster who had been elected to represent the opposition element of the Des Moines Conference, were both expelled from the Board of Trustees for their opposition to the interests of the college and the regulations of the board. Thus ingloriously ended the scheme of fraud which rebellion and treason had planned. Indeed

"The best laid plans of mice and men
Aft gang aglee."

THE CHURCH IN ST. PAUL, MINN.

The attention of the reader is next directed to the attempt to steal our fine church property in St. Paul, Minn., probably worth $30,000.00. The scheme was inaugurated by a resolution of the Board of Trustees of said Church declaring the suspension of Bishops Esher and Bowman to have been valid, and that therefore they could not be recognized as bishops. These resolutions furthermore declared that in the opinion of these trustees Rudolph Dubs was a very pious man, and expressed sympathy with him for the martyrdom he was suffering. They also declared that they would receive no one as their minister except the person mentioned in their resolutions. A copy of these resolutions was sent to the Annual Conference. The Church in question had been built by funds collected by canvassing the entire conference district, and the preachers of the conference had themselves personally contributed very liberally. Yet these trustees had placed a mortgage upon the Church without requesting permission of the conference to do so. When their attention was called to this matter by the P. E., Bro. Linse, they declared they needed no authority from conference and could get along without it.

Soon after the conference session above named meetings of the congregations were very frequently held, evidently for the purpose of prejudicing the membership against the authorities of the Church, so as to make their plans more easy of accomplishment. The presiding elder found that the congregation itself was in reality loyal to the Church and that the agitation was carried on by a few persons in the interest of Dubs' rebellion. Among these was a man, comparatively young but the possessor of unbounded egotism and a towering "bump" of self-esteem, who in some manner had gained almost complete control of affairs. He hailed from Chicago where it seems he had been well instructed by the "ring." This man and another fitting associate, also from Chicago, circulated a petition forbidding the use of the pulpit to the presiding elder. This and other circumstances which had plainly indicated the purpose in view finally induced the P. E. to carry out the instructions received at conference by bringing charges against the two persons spoken of above, and two of the trustees. The charges were placed in the hands of Rev. J. G. Simon, the P. E. of the adjacent district, who immediately took steps to bring them to trial. When the committee which had been selected met, and the trial was about to commence, an officer of the law appeared

ATTEMPTS TO ALIENATE CHURCH PROPERTY. 165

on the scene notifying all concerned that the court had granted an injunction restraining the Church tribunal from proceeding in the case. One of the pleas used to secure the injunction was that the accused had given their individual obligations for a large amount of the debt of the Church, and that if they were expelled they would suffer great financial loss. This took place in July. The Judges soon afterward took their Summer vacation so that no hearing on a motion to dissolve the injunction could be secured. This afforded the rebellions element time to mature and carry out their plans. On the following Sabbath an announcement was made that on Monday, August 18th, a meeting of the congregation would be held in order to authorize the trustees to sell the Church. This at once uncovered the plot. Rev. J. L. Stegner, the pastor of the Church, and Rev. C. Brill, a retired minister, now saw the real purpose of those men, and also took a stand with the P. E., Bro. H. E. Linse, against the scheme. Up to this time they had both more or less sympathized with the agitators, but their sense of duty and loyalty to their vows as ministers and their honor as men, would not allow them to be partners in such a wicked conspiracy. Brother Stegner, the pastor therefore publicly protested against the call for such a meeting, on the ground that it was illegal and wrong. During the time intervening between the announcement and the meeting of the congregation, which in accordance with the laws of the State had to be announced for two Sabbaths in succession, it became known that a society had already been incorporated, consisting of seven individuals, one a member of our Church, four members of the M. E. Church, and two persons who were not members of any church, under the name and title of "The United Evangelical Church of St. Paul, Minn." The notice for such an incorporation had been inserted in a small Roman Catholic paper, and as a matter of course none of our members had seen it. But Bro. Linse and our loyal people were also at work, and through Mr. Fitzpatrick of St. Paul, and Mr. E. B. Esher of Chicago, a temporary injunction was secured restraining the congregation from selling the property. Notice had been served upon several of the principal conspirators. Three, however, succeeded in secreting themselves and therefore had not been served. Nevertheless on the Sabbath morning previous to the congregational meeting which had been called to sell the Church property, some one who was no official of the Church, came to the services and notwithstanding the protest of the P. E., Rev. H. E. Linse, and notwithstanding the latter's statement that a temporary injunction had been issued by the court restraining the congregation from taking any further action, this person read what purported to be a notice to the congregation to meet the following evening. On the following Monday evening some people gathered in the Church, Bro. Linse was not allowed to enter although he was the Presiding Elder, and as such had the oversight of the temporal as well as the spiritual affairs of the Churches in his district, upon the ground that he was no member of the congregation. The pastor, Bro. J. L. Stegner, was not allowed to preside, nor was he permitted to speak. A president was elected, a motion made to authorize the Trustees to sell the church property of the Immanuel Church of the Evangelical Association to the "United Evangelical Church of St. Paul" for the sum of *ten dollars!* A property probably worth $30,000 sold for $10 to seven persons, one a member of our Church, four members of the M. E. Church, and two belonging to no Church! Moreover a property secured by the united efforts of the entire Minnesota Conference. The resolution authorizing the sale was adopted in great haste. The deed had been previously written, and the Trustees who had kept themselves in hiding so the Sheriff could not serve the writ of injunction upon them, were brought from their hiding-places during the night, and the deed executed. The next day the deed was taken to the registry office and ordered to be put on record, and these Dubsites considered the clandestine transfer of the property of the Church accomplished. In order to keep the pastor and our loyal people out of the church on the following Sunday they now barricaded the doors and secured the windows. During the week no services could be held. Bro. Stegner was heroic enough not to be easily kept out of his pulpit. With the aid of several loyal brethren he effected an entrance into the church, removed the barricades, and put a new lock on the door. The sexton who lived in the basement of the church, was, however, in full sympathy with the rebellious clique, so that through him Bro. Stegner's plans were after all thwarted and the thieves held possession of the church. On Sunday morning there was no service in the church, but in the afternoon C. A. Paeth, a former disloyal professor in the U. B. Institute, and at this time a Dubsite minister in Chicago, preached in the church. This man was the secretary of the rump conference in Philadelphia, Pa., another link which binds this dishonorable and dishonest piece of business to the Dubs rebellion and secession. Meanwhile strong efforts were made by these parties to induce Bro. Stegner to join their ranks and become the pastor of the new corporation. Every possible inducement was held out. One of the Dubsites from Chicago even attempted the regulation Dubs measure of shedding tears in his attempt to induce Bro. Stegner to break his vows and become a traitor to his Church. However, Bro. Stegner stood firm. Not succeeding in this manner, their friendship for Bro. Stegner underwent a rapid change, and they secured an injunction principally directed against him for breaking into their church! This was injunction No. 3. So now Bro. Stegner was effectually barred out of his pulpit. During the following week there was no service in the church, but on the following Sunday a German Methodist minister, who knew all the facts, and who was requested by Bro. Stegner not to occupy his pulpit under the circumstances, preached in the church, and thus not only showed a great lack of courtesy for the pastor, and great disrepect for our Church, but also made himself a partaker of other men's sins. At this service a congregational meeting of the "new church" was called in order to authorize the Trustees to make a loan of $1,500 on some vacant lots owned by the congregation in the northern part of the city, in order to pay the legal expenses incurred in stealing the property of the Evangelical Association ! It was now our turn to secure an injunction restraining them from encumbering the property. The injunction was promptly secured not only against the seven original conspirators, but also against twenty-eight others who had united with them. This last injunction locked up the church completely. They were not allowed under its wording to use the church for any purpose.

On the 10th of September the whole matter came up before the court on a motion to dissolve the injunctions. Injunction No. 1 restraining Bro. Linse from proceeding with the charges was dissolved in about fifteen minutes, and the plaintiffs ordered to pay the costs. The other injunctions occupied the attention of the court about a day and a half, Judge Kelley, a very able jurist, presiding. One of the counsel for the conspirators admitted that if the presentation of facts made to the Court was correct, his clients were guilty of contempt and might be severely punished. He soon afterwards entirely withdrew from the case. Several days later the Judge rendered his decision, dissolving the two injunctions obtained against the church, while the temporary injunctions obtained against the Dubsites were made permanent, and the property of the church again put into the hands of its rightful owners. The deed which had been made under such false pretenses was annulled and set aside by the Court, and thus also ingloriously ended this attempt of alienating the property of the church at St. Paul.

Of course after the injunction against the trial of several of the conspirators was dissolved the trial was held and they were expelled from the church. Others withdrew, and now since these agitators and dishonest followers of Dubs are gone, peace and prosperity attends the church. Just as affairs of the Publishing House are prospering in peace since the agitators are gone ; just as there is harmony in the college at Naperville since the Dubsites are all out of it ; just as there is peace in Japan since we are delivered from the evil spirit which Dubsism constantly cultivated; so there is peace in our St. Paul congregation since Dubs' followers have left. There can be no peace where its spirit can make itself felt.

Much credit is due Bro. H. E. Linse for his firmness and decision and the prudence manifested in the difficulties in the St. Paul society. Bro. C. Brill, who has since entered the Church Triumphant, also stood up firmly and nobly when he discovered the plans of the conspirators.

FORGING A DEED.

The third item in this sad history of attempts to take away by any means, fair or foul, the property of the Church, an attempt of forgery must be noticed. The Dubsites commenced proceedings in Tazewell Co., Ill., against Rev. W. Neitz and Rev. E. R. Troyer, as presiding elder and preacher in charge of our church at Washington, Ill., the same church in which Dubs had made a public declaration of war against Bishop Esher, eighteen months after his election as bishop. The proceedings were commenced by F. Busse and J. H. Schultze. The attorneys for the Church had several times asked permission during the course of the trial to examine the original deed, which was in the hands of the seceders, but instead of being given the original, they always received what purported to be a copy. Finally, however, Mr. E. B. Esher managed to get the original deed into his hands, and upon examination discovered that a forgery had been committed by some one. Before he had time to apprise anyone of his discovery, F. Busse, who was present and saw Mr. Esher examine the deed, exclaimed, "I didn't do it." Consequently he knew that the deed had been changed and considered it worth the while to deny being guilty of the act before anyone charged him with it!

The deed is in the handwriting of our sainted Bishop Long, and was of course written so as to secure the property for the Church. The trust clause reads as follows: "And in further trust and confidence that they shall at all times forever hereafter permit such ministers and preachers belonging to the said Evangelical Association as shall from time to time be duly authorized by the General Conference or by the annual conferences authorized by the said General Conference to preach and expound God's holy Word therein." In this citation the word "General" had been erased and "annual" inserted in its stead. The purpose of Bishop Long was to secure this property for the Church, hence says, "such annual conferences as may be authorized by the General Conference," and such preachers "as shall be duly authorized by General Conference." Bishop Long, as may be readily seen, did not hold to the heresy that the General Conference is subordinate to the annual conferences, but that our Church is one and its government is centralized in the General Conference. Dubsism has attempted to reverse this order, hence this clumsy forgery. Judge Smith in his opinion rendered in the injunction granted against the Church in the Naperville case had given expression to this heresy, holding that the decisions and acts of the annual conferences were binding upon the courts, hence the person who committed this forgery doubtless thought that if the deed would recognize the annual conference only they would as a matter of course get possession of the church in question. Presumably also the person guilty of this crime had heard Bishop Dubs' "masterpiece" of a speech delivered in this church in which he appealed to "the great Illinois Conference" to arise in behalf of an institution of the Church owned and managed by quite a number of conferences, hence the rights of an annual conference were greatly magnified in the mind of this forger, leading him to suppose that if he could make the deed read in accordance with these ideas victory was certain.

The Dubsites tried their utmost to wash their hands of this stupid crime, but facts are hard things to get rid of.

1. The deed was in their possession. 2. The forgery was in accord with their doctrine. 3. The forgery was in their interest.

4. They were perfectly quiet about the matter until it was discovered. 5. They attempted to prevent a discovery of the crime by keeping the deed away from our attorneys. 6. They were greatly excited when the discovery was made. 7. They attempted to justify the meanness and explain it away as a small matter.

Certainly Dubsism has been compelled to " stoop " in order to conquer. " This rebellion was conceived in iniquity, brought forth in depravity, raised in corruption, and has contaminated every man prominently connected with it."

IN THE IOWA CONFERENCE.

The first indication of trouble in this conference was a report to the effect that all articles of incorporation of religious societies in Iowa would lapse in twenty years. Hence it was said all our oldest societies must be re-incorporated immediately, and many others very soon. With this report the question was coupled : " Can not our societies own and control their church property themselves and in their own name, independent of the annual conference ? " The spreading of the report above mentioned, connected with the agitation of being independent, caused a great deal of uneasiness among the loyal people and ministers, so that an attorney was consulted in reference to the matter. He assured us that re-incorporation was not necessary according to the law of the State. This fact convinced our loyal ministers that some underground work was being done for some specific purpose. The sequel showed that herein they were not mistaken.

At this time Rev. J. Henn had charge of Ackley District. The society at Ackley, where Mr. Henn had resided for some years, was about to build a new church. A preliminary meeting of the society was held, presided over by the pastor, Rev. F. Beltzer. Mr. Henn was also present. The question was raised by one who has always been an adherent of the rebellion and secession of R. Dubs & Co., whether the articles of incorporation of the society would not lapse at the end of twenty years.

Beltzer referred the question to the presiding elder, who answered in the affirmative, adding that the present articles would very soon be of no effect, and new ones must be drawn up. Then the question was raised whether if new articles of incorporation must be made they could not be made so that the society would control its own property.

This question was also referred to Mr. Henn for an answer by Rev. F. Beltzer. Henn's answer was that it might be "fixed" in that way, stating further that one of our societies in Baltimore, Md., and one in Philadelphia, Pa., were incorporated in their own name and controlled their property independently. As a result of this opinion and advice of the presiding elder, whose duty as such would have been to protect the interests of the conference which had entrusted him with this influential office, articles of incorporation were adopted which were not in harmony with our Discipline.

Later on Mr. Henn made the same statements above referred to on various fields of labor on his district, adding that our society in Ackley on his district had also been thus incorporated. Valentine Griese, another minister of the Iowa Conference, who was afterwards suspended by the conference for his rebellious conduct at the opening of the conference session in Ackley, Ia., in 1890, had prevailed upon the Quarterly Conference to order new articles of incorporation for our society at Luverne, Ia., because as he stated the original articles had not been acknowledged and hence were void.

When afterwards Mr. Henn came to the charge as P. E. early in 1890, the articles of incorporation of the society in Luverne were placed into his hands for examination. He struck therefrom every reference to the Evangelical Association, and the annual and General Conference, as well as the Discipline of the Church, and adding thereto several items, thereby completely severing the society from the Evangelical Association, making the society in all respects entirely independent without any ecclesiastical connection with any denomination. This worthy (?)

and loyal (?) P. E. then instructed the preacher in charge to copy the articles as changed by him, *and burn the original*, which he had changed. The reader will no doubt draw his own inference and conclusions. A copy of the changed articles was afterwards submitted to the Trustees of the society at Luverne for their adoption. However, upon examination, finding that they would be cut loose from the Evangelical Association, they refused to sign the treasonable document, and Henn's disloyal plans were frustrated. Henn himself acknowledged to a brother that his purpose was to make the society independent. And as it was necessary for certain reasons to have a new deed executed for the church property to the new incorporation, Henn's plan, had it succeeded, would have been quite effectual, indeed.

At Hampton, also in Mr. Henn's district, the workings of the same dishonest scheme are met with. The Society was about to acquire a new and very valuable church property. Mr. Henn felt it to be his duty to be present and advise how to proceed to secure the church property, and finally he dictated Articles of Incorporation exactly like those he had "fixed" for our people at Luverne, cutting the society and the property loose from the Evangelical Association. However this attempt on the part of the P. E., to divert the property of the Church was also frustrated. And notwithstanding this treachery and gross violation of his vows as a minister of our Church, this man all along claimed to be loyal, and pretends to be hurt when the facts of his treason are presented. In some localities the base work succeeded. At Ackley, the circumstances have already been given, the papers under Henn and Beltzer's supervision and management are not in accordance with our Discipline. The fact that Beltzer was disloyal to the Church was no doubt well known to the conspirators in Illinois, hence he was called to sit in the mock trial held in Chicago of one of the bishops. The leaders always knew their men. The congregation, however, at Ackley remained loyal, hence the plan did not avail much after all. At Floyd and Lemars, however, the plan succeeded and the secessionists now hold the property of the Church. At Sioux City the Iowa Conference furnished $7,000.00 to purchase the lot and build the church. The property is deeded to the Iowa Conference, but under the influence of a disloyal minister, the Society seceded from the Iowa Conference which furnished the large amount of money above named, and united with the Kooker-Utt "Conference," clearly against the law of our Church, and a preacher so-called, occupies the Church, held not only as usual in trust for the conference, but owned by it directly. Legal proceedings have been instituted by the Iowa Conference which are still pending in the courts. The case carried to the Supreme Court of the State from the decision of Judge Conrad in Des Moines, will also virtually decide this case.

At Lemars, Rev. H. Kleinsorge, who had acccepted an appointment from the Iowa Conference, and signed its proceedings as a token of acquiescence and obedience, also soon after his arrival on the charge, signed the same kind of articles drawn up after the Henn pattern, severing the society from the Evangelical Association. Moreover, he made strong and repeated efforts to induce the person who had formerly executed a deed for the parsonage to execute a new deed which would grant the property to the newly formed independent incorporation, in order, fully, as he thought, to secure the property so it could be used by the rebellious preachers. And yet this man, like Henn, still claims to be a Christian minister and preaches the Word which says: Thou shalt not steal. The person in question, however, decidedly refused to sign a new deed, although Kleinsorge mailed a deed written out and ready to be signed and acknowledged, and offered to pay him if he would sign it.

Although Kleinsorge thus faithfully served the Dubsites, he was nevertheless compelled to leave Lemars already in the Fall of the same year, in order that one more acceptable to the independent society could take his place. This of course will be the experience a good many more of these secession preachers will make in the near future. Societies which control their own property, will also control the pulpit, and say who and who shall not use the same. He then went to Stanton, nine miles distant, and without any show of authority took possession of the Church and parsonage, even against explicit warnings, even refusing the authorized minister the use of the Church at such times as he and his followers did not use it. These are the people who now cry out so lustily against the Church for taking possession of its churches after the courts have decided that she has the exclusive right to her property. Kleinsorge held the property illegally and unjustly until he was compelled to vacate by an order from the court. Then, although compelled to vacate the property to the use of which he had no vestige of right, he writes to the German organ of his faction, that he acted in accordance with the Scriptural injunction: "If any man will sue thee at the law, and take away thy coat, let him have thy cloak also." Has such a man any conscience left? Is it not blasphemy to use the Word of God in such a manner?

On Otter Creek charge through the manipulation of J. Beltzer and William Jonas, two different meetings were held in the Fall of 1890, controlled by Jonas, without any vestige of ecclesiastical authority, in which Articles of Incorporation were forced upon the people, adopted by a bare majority, some of the signers who were not conversant with the English language, having been induced to sign the document under the pretence that they were signing a paper which was intended to avoid difficulty, and the purpose of which was to leave things just as they had been. And yet the articles were drawn up after the Henn pattern, which made the Society entirely independent of the Evangelical Association. Soon after these new Articles of Incorporation had been adopted, which as Jonas and Beltzer alleged were made to avoid trouble, and leave everything as it had been, two of the trustees placed a strong lock on the door of the Church, and a notice upon the door notifying the preacher in charge in this very brotherly manner: "We have hereafter no further use for you, and have this day locked the doors of the Church against you." These two trustees add the name of a third who had said, "Macht was ihr wollt"—do as you please. The following Sunday the doors were locked against the legal pastor and presiding elder, and some of the former members, and some who never had been members, with the hireling preachers, held service, and when they left they securely guarded the church against the legal pastor and members of the Church. This is the honesty of Dubsism. However, the way of the transgressors is not easy. During the following week E. B. Esher secured an injunction against these church robbers from Judge Preston, of Cedar Rapids, and their scheme was ended.

By some oversight no deed had been made for our parsonage at Odebolt, Ia. Previous to 1887, before R. Dubs had decided to divide the Church in his interest, he presided at a Quarterly Conference held on this charge. He not only presided, but also acted as secretary at the same time. He insisted that the society must incorporate at once and see to it that a deed was executed, suggesting a strong resolution to that effect, which appears on the records in his own handwriting. However, the resolutions were not carried out. In 1891, Wm. Jonas, one of Dubs' henchmen, to aid in diverting church property, appears on the scene. He gets together from various appointments on the mission, five persons, and gets them to sign incorporation papers after Henn's pattern, has them acknowledged, and recorded. Then he goes to the person from whom the ground had been purchased, but who had neglected to execute a deed, and induces him to make a deed to the new incorporation. This parsonage has since been occupied by the rebel minister in defiance of all moral right.

At Charles City, Iowa, Emil Mueller had been stationed by the Iowa Conference in 1888, being to a large extent supported by the missionary funds of the conference. A church and parsonage were built towards which liberal amounts were furnished by the conference. The deed, etc., were sent to the conference for examination and approval, and were accepted. Not so very long afterwards this same Mueller presents "amended" articles of incorporation much after Henn's pattern, entirely separating the congregation from the Evangelical Association. He manages to have them adopted by the congregation, and has them recorded. Now everything is ready. No one but he and his willing dupes know anything about it, so the Trustees of Zion Church of the Evangelical Association, the original incorporation as created by the charter and approved by the conference, do " sell and convey " to themselves naming the Trustees of the new and independent organization such as the amended articles, presented by the treacherous Mueller, had created, or at least pretended to create, thus transferring the valuable church property for the consideration of one dollar! However, it seems they still had sense enough left to feel that after all such a proceeding would hardly stand the test of law, hence some other plan is agreed upon. A mortage is executed, *at ninety days after date*, and placed upon the property. As soon as the three months are expired, foreclosure proceedings are commenced immediately. However, the Sheriff notifies the Trustees of the Iowa Conference, who appear in court, and after a full hearing the Court sets the mortgage aside and all proceedings under it as illegal, so that part of the theft is hindered by the strong arm of the law. Still to this day they illegally and unjustly have the property of the Church in their possession and use. Whenever the case pending in court for restoration of the property was to be tried they came loaded with affidavits that they were unable to proceed with the trial of the case!

It would be but a repetition of the same dishonest methods and work to describe the manner in which they secured possession of the property of the Church in Nora Springs, Newburg, Defiance and Rockwell City, so that for the sake of brevity they are passed over.

All this downright robbery has been participated in by the followers of R. Dubs to get away with the property of the Evangelical Association. It seems most incredible that men professing to be Christians could be guilty of such gross dishonesty. They have evidently adopted the Popish principle, "The end justifies the means."

As evidence that the changes in title deeds and corporation papers made as herein stated was done to divert the property of the Church, the statement of Rev. F. Benz, a minister of the Iowa Conference, at present stationed in Fort Dodge, Iowa, is attached:

"Whereas up to the conference session in Ackley, Iowa, in 1890, I had full confidence in the righteousness, and hence ultimate victory of the cause of the 'minority,' and had expressed myself on this wise to both friend and foe. However, the plan of the leaders to retreat into the Congregational Church had not been divulged to me up to that time. But when in Ackley I saw the cause of the 'minority' was so righteously defeated by the grace of God, and I expressed my doubts as to the final outcome, I was consoled and exhorted to be content, and courageously to continue the fight, and if all should fail to keep myself ready to unite with the Congregational Church, or to go elsewhere. From this I learned that the leaders, whose conduct at that conference seemed very questionable to me, had no faith in their cause, and that they purposed to introduce a despotism of deception and falsehood.

"Soon after the conference session, I think it was in May, 1890, I received an invitation to come to Des Moines, Iowa, to meet with others of the alienated and disobedient sons of the Iowa Conference and to confer with the Congregational State Association in reference to uniting with that Church. I remained away, and only know what transpired at the meeting as far as J. Henn, who was my Presiding Elder, told me at the next Quarterly Conference. He said: '*The Congregationalists are willing to help us and receive us,*' etc. That Henn & Co. did not go away sooner was not their fault, for they have long since been anything else but Evangelical.

"[Signed]   F. BENZ."

THE ATTEMPT TO ALIENATE THE EBENEZER CHURCH OF THE EVANGELICAL ASSOCIATION IN ALLENTOWN, PA.

The above church was built about 1868 or 1869, and dedicated in accordance with the ritual of our Church by Rev. Thomas Bowman and Rev. Jesse Yeakel, then P. E. of the district, at the request of the pastor and trustees. The deed had been executed October 9, 1868, by Moses Schadt and wife, conveying the lot upon which the church was built to W. F. Christman, Perry Wannemacher, H. S. Weaver and George H. Good as trustees, and contained the clause in our Discipline, declaring the same to be in trust for the ministry and membership of the Evangelical Association. About the same time a charter was granted by the Court of Common Pleas of Lehigh Co., incorporating the society as the Ebenezer Church of the Evangelical Association. Article IV. of the charter provides " that the Trustees shall suffer and permit at all times hereafter the ministers and preachers belonging to the religious society called the Evangelical Association, who shall be duly authorized and appointed by the annual conference to preach and expound the Word of God, and in all things manage and control the said church and execute this trust according to the rules and Discipline of the said Association." Article V. authorized the Trustees to borrow money for the use of the church, not exceeding $3,000, and to mortgage the church property for the same.

In 1889 the old church was removed to another lot, and a new church erected upon the old site. Then after the conference session in Shamokin, Pa., where the purposes of the majority of the East Pa. Conference became known, a scheme was entered into by some of the laymen of the society and the disloyal ministers of the conference, chief of whom was W. F. Heil, to alienate this valuable property from the Church. Hence on April 5, 1890, Moses Schadt and wife made and executed another deed for the same lot, but including five feet more in width on Turner Street than the deed of 1868 called for. In the mean time Mr.

Schadt had become insolvent and could not for that reason own any real estate and execute a clear title. The adjoining property formerly owned by Mr. Schadt had long since passed out of his hands, and as the first deed called for so many feet more or less, the reason assigned for executing a new deed for property sold twenty-two years previous bore fraud upon its very face. In this new deed Moses B. Schadt and wife conveyed the same property for which they had executed a deed in trust to the Trustees above named twenty-two years previous to "the Ebenezer Church of the Evangelical Association of the city of Allentown, Pa." In this new deed the statement is inserted that the trust clause was "inadvertently inserted" in the original deed.

On April 22, 1890, a petition signed by the Trustees of this church was presented to the Court to have the charter amended.

In the rebuilding of this church it was found that they would have to borrow more money than the old charter allowed, and in order to obtain the requisite authority to do so, Rev. A. Krecker, during the year of 1889, called a meeting of the congregation, and a resolution was passed to the effect that an application should be made to the Court for an amendment to the charter authorizing the Trustees to borrow $12,000.00. *No other amendment was mentioned at this meeting or authorized by the congregation.* But the articles of amendment presented to the Court among other things contained the following: "Said corporation is desirous of improving, amending, and altering the articles and conditions of the said charter and at a meeting of said congregation, duly convened, the following improvements, amendments, and alterations of the said charter were duly adadopted. 1st. The name of the Corporation shall be the Ebenzer Evangelical Congregation. 2nd. The purpose for which the corporation is formed is the support of public worship. 3rd. That so much of Article III. of the instrument or articles of Association under which the said corporation was incorporated, reading as follows: 'And shall suffer and permit at all times hereafter the ministers belonging to the Religious Society called the Evangelical Association who shall be duly authorized by the annual conference to preach and expound the Word of God therein, and in all things manage and control the said church and execute this trust according to the rules and Discipline of association,' *be amended, canceled, and made void.* 4th. Contained the amendment in reference to the change from $3,000.00 to $12,000.00 as stated above. 5th. That Article VI. of said instrument or Articles of Association reading as follows : ' The said Trustees shall have power to pass by-laws and regulations necessary to carry the articles into effect not contrary to the rules and regulations and Discipline of the Evangelical Association, be amended and altered so as to read. The members of this corporation shall have power to make by-laws for the government of said corporation and alter and amend the same from time to time provided the same be not contrary to the constitution and laws of this commonwealth. Then after another clause came the following: "All property, real or personal which the said corporation now owns, or which shall hereafter be bequeathed, or devised, or conveyed to the same shall be taken and held subject to the control and disposition of the lay members thereof, or such constituted officers, representatives thereof, as shall be composed of a majority of lay members." The reader will notice that just as J. Henn struck out all reference to the Evangelical Association in the amended charters in Iowa, so it was done in this case. With this difference that after all Mr. Henn was honest enough to let the people know his plans, while in this case an attempt was made to have the charter revised, alienating the Society absolutely and entirely from the Church in an under-handed and glaringly dishonest manner. These amendments had not been presented to the congregation previous to making application to the Court, and only those who were in the secret knew of it. The others believing the only amendment was the financial change. The reason for this secret deed of darkness is apparent. There was an influential minority in the congregation, led by Bro. Loux, Bro. Yeager,

Bro. Wieand, Bro. Peters and others, who could neither be driven, nor coaxed, nor persecuted into rebellion, nor into secession from the Evangelical Association, *and their money was needed*, hence they were to be defrauded out of their rights.

The amendments to the charter were granted by the Court on June 30, 1890 ; but it seems their lawyers discovered that the amendments had not been authorized by the Society, and had been procured without the knowledge or consent of the same, hence they knew of course that they were wholly invalid and of none effect. So they advised these conspirators to have the amendments ratified by the Society. A meeting for this purpose was called by Rev. J. W. Hoover, who was then the pastor for Sept. 3, 1890, and an attempt made to ratify the amendments without having them read, but Bro. T. L. Wieand and the others mentioned objected so strenuously that the plan did not succeed. Another meeting was called on Sept. 22nd, 1890, at this meeting, one of the chief rebels of the East, W. F. Heil, was present and encouraged his adherents to go forward in their work. There were about 130 present of a membership of 400, and finally a majority of these voted to ratify the fraudulent charter. Bro. Wieand earnestly protested, but was declared out of order by Heil, although some one else presided.

The parties guilty of such an unwarranted assumption of power, who thus override the guaranteed rights of others, and arrogate unto themselves the authority to do just as they please, are the ones who make the outcry against tyranny and despotism. It really seems incredible that men who in ordinary business transactions have the reputation of honesty can in such matters trample every principle of equity and justice under their feet. Yet such is the sad fact. Still this bold attempt to alienate this valuable property from the church will fail most ingloriously. The second deed executed by Moses Schadt and wife is not worth the paper it is written upon, and the Ebenezer Church in Allentown, Pa., is still in spite of the charter, which was obtained in such a dishonorable way, the property of the Evangelical Association.

Other attempts have been made to get away with the property of the church, but space does not allow any more details to be given. Why these attempts to alienate the property of the church if, as Heil, and all the rest of Dubs' tools in the East as well as elsewhere claim, they are the Evangelical Association? These very attempts will give the lie to their pretensions.

CHAPTER XI.

The Harvest.

The harvest has been fearful and the end is not yet. Seven annual conferences have been torn asunder in the interests of R. Dubs and his followers. Several of these, the Des Moines, the Platte River, and the Oregon, have been mission conferences from the organization to the time of their disruption and have cost the church thousands of dollars. Congregations almost without number have been torn asunder, families have been divided against themselves, Sunday-schools disrupted, life-long friends separated, and ill-feeling and bitterness engendered which perhaps in this world will not be wholly overcome. Not a few ministers and laymen have gone into eternity in the frame of mind brought about by these things. And why? Indeed echo answers why? Hon. J. Winslow Wood, the Master in the chancery cases in Allentown, Pa., who probably inquired more thoroughly into all the facts connected with the history of these difficulties than any other, says: "There is no sufficient cause, absolutely none, for the distraction in this church." Repeatedly have the leaders been challenged to set up their case and give the reasons for all these troubles. To this day they have not done it. It cannot be done. After reading the facts presented in this volume can any one still condemn the church for re-calling Jacob Hartzler? If any blame can be attached to the church it is that he was ever sent to Japan, and after his incompetency became so apparent that he was still allowed to remain. Will it not be an unexplained mystery to the future historian of our church that H. B. Hartzler was endured so long in the editorial chair after he had declared war upon the church and her authorities? Even if these men had not been properly dealt with, if the church had erred in its judgment, would that have been a sufficient reason for causing all this sorrow and distruction? Neither of them was deposed from the office of the ministry. Both of them might have continued to labor in spheres for which they were fitted in their own or some other annual conference. It was very evident that they were utterly unfitted for the positions with which the church had entrusted them. And after reading the facts presented in this volume in connection with the conduct and character of R. Dubs (and these facts cannot be successfully contradicted, but much more might have been added), is it seemly that for his sake all this ruin of a church which God had signally blessed, should be wrought? He never was morally fit for the place with which the church honored him, and as years went by he became thoroughly and in all probability hopelessly corrupt.

"However," the tyranny and despotism of Bishops Esher and Bowman" has not been mentioned. This revolt is against their enslavement of the church, and the terrible" yoke, they have forced the church to bear." This ridiculous cry is so absurd that it taxes one's patience to reply to the absurdity. In a church where the office of Bishop expires every four years, where he must be re-elected by ballot, and must receive, in order to be elected, a majority of all the votes cast, where the ballot is absolutely secret, it sounds boyish and actually foolish, to prate about episcopal tyranny and despotism. No one in his sober senses believes that if Bishop Esher was the "pope" and "despot" and "tyrant" these men in their desperation to justify their rebellious course have pictured him, he would have been re-elected eight times in succession, and at the last General Conference practically unanimously? While it is admitted that in the extraordinary scenes through which we have passed in dealing with this gigantic conspiracy extending from the Atlantic to the Pacific and even into Japan, it became necessary on several occasions to make use of extreme measures, such as no one would think of using in ordinary times and under ordinary circumstances. They were wartimes through which the church passed. The hope is sincerely entertained that such occasions and such scenes may never again return. However, where, or when, or under what circumstances was either Bishop Esher or the writer guilty of any act or measure, previous to the full outbreak of the rebellion, and the attempt to disorganize the church, which has even the semblance of tyranny or despotism? This whole outcry is utterly unfounded, and has been made simply to prejudice the people and lead them astray and cover up the real purpose of the seceders. Its authors well knew that such a cry would go far with the liberty loving American people to aid them in their designs. There was neither truth nor sense in it. If ever our church had a bishop who tried to rule and who did rule with arrogance and intimidation, until the uncovering of his life and real character turned his arrogance into cowardice, it was Rudolph Dubs, and his followers know this statement to be correct.

The scenes enacted by the seceders at the annual conferences which they divided by their lawlessness are so fresh in the minds of our readers that it is unnecessary to enter into details in this volume. Those who witnessed the sad scene at the Sheffield Avenue Church in the city of Chicago well remember when Bishop J. J. Esher, who had been a member of the Illinois Conference since its organization, who had done more to build up the work in the bounds of that conference than all his enemies put together, whose character for integrity and veracity was unimpeachable, who had been a Bishop of the Church for twenty-six years in succession, and during this time had organized many new conferences in this and foreign lands, is refused admittance into a church of the Evangelical Association by several individuals who guard the door, one of them actually under the influence of liquor, at the behest of John Schneider, William Huelster and others equally as wicked! Talk about the assumption of power by the Bishops as compared with such a piece of tyranny and despotism exercised without the shadow of any authority. Talk about a bishop suspending a minister or two who misbehave themselvs as compared with such an assumption of power for which there is no trace of warrant in our Discipline or any other law, to say nothing of its reprehensible meanness.

A scene almost similar to this was enacted at the Turner St. Church in the city of Allentown, Pa. There the door was not only guarded, but the church had been barricaded and watched all night previous, while the Bishop was peacefully sleeping in the house of Bro. T. L. Wieand on 9th St. in that city. The ministers in Chicago it seems after all commissioned the reprehensible work of thrusting the Bishop out of the church to several laymen. Even one of these hardly considered himself capable to perform such a duty without first nerving himself with whiskey. But in Allentown, Pa., actually two men calling themselves ministers, possibly not trusting their lay brethren, as these were at least sober, took it upon themselves to guard the door, and to tell the Bishop, "You can't come in." As to these two individuals, the writer's pen almost revolts against writing their names, and yet it must go down into history that W. F. Heil and A. M. Sampeel were mean enough and wicked enough to stoop to such wretched work. They may not have been drunk with sweet wine, but they were fairly drunk with self-conceit with the success, as they imagined, of the conspiracy into which they had entered with others at a secret meeting held several months previous in Reading, Pa.

The disturbances which this unruly element made at Ackley, Iowa, and at Albany, Oregon, were in some respects even more disgraceful and sinful, because they were enacted in the house of God consecrated to divine worship. The writer had been in Ackley at least twenty-four hours previous to the opening of the conference session. Mr. Henn, the leader of the opposition, lived in Ackley, and all the rest were there the day previous. They all knew where the writer roomed, but not a single one of them called to see him, if possible, to make some arrangements by which a disturbance in the house of God might be avoided. The writer did not have the least intimation from them that they would object to his presiding. Privately, previous to the opening of the session, there would probably have been no difficulty to arrange matters in a manner which would have obviated a disturbance. When in the chair as Bishop of the Evangelical Association no stipulations or compromise was possible. Then the writer was the official representative of his church and would have died rather than compromise his personal or official integrity. At Ackley the doors could not be locked against the bishop as the majority of the Board of Trustees were loyal men and true. When about to open the conference with the usual devotional exercises, Valentine Griesse, H. Lageschulte, Jacob Henn, and others, who had united with them in their conspiracy entered into a secret meeting held a day or two previous, created such a disturbance as will for all time to come be a personal disgrace for them and their wicked cause. The writer has often thanked God for his sustaining grace in that trying ordeal and for the Divine help and inspiration with which those unscrupulous men were subdued into quietness, and the Iowa Conference saved intact for the Evangelical Association. The abuse and persecution received since by the writer for the course he was compelled to adopt, has had very little effect other than to strengthen him in the conviction that his course stands approved by God as well as the church.

At Albany, Oregon, J. Bowersox, C. C. Poling, and those who acted with them not only grievously sinned against the law of God, but the law of common decency as well, and in addition to the reprehensible act as professed ministers of disturbing public worship, they deliberately again and again made false statements—statements they knew were false when they made them, and in a most shameless manner slandered the writer, some of them even swearing to their false statements in courts of equity. No wonder disaster has followed them ever since, and the displeasure of God has visibly rested upon them. That they have not been cut down in their iniquity is only another evidence of the long-suffering of God. Josiah Bowersox, who had been one of the presiding elders, had arranged a series of appointments for the writer after the conference session, had announced a dedication for me, and even the previous week he had written to San Francisco, Cal., expressing regret that he could not arrange another dedication in time for me. Soon after the writer's arrival in Oregon he called at his rooms and bade him welcome to Oregon. In the annual missionary meeting he took a seat besides the bishop and planned how best to reach the appointments after the session. He accompanied the writer to his room in the evening and aided in arranging the committees for the conference session, and incidentally also the boundaries were discussed. Bowersox neither by word nor deed intimated that there might be trouble or that anything was wrong. The next morning this man Bowersox was one of the worst in the excited crowd, and has since shown himself a worthy follower of R. Dubs in the line of untruthfulness. It can be proven by at least four respectable witnesses, whose testimony cannot be impeached that Bowersox told them it was not true that the writer laid violent hands upon him, and yet in order to serve his party he swore that this gross slander was true. What is a man, capable of such treachery, not capable of doing? For years this man was paid a good salary out of the Missionary Treasury and then plays the traitor to his church.

Nor are these things the only bitter fruit which has grown out of this causeless and wicked rebellion. The sad fact that these parties dragged the church before the civil courts brought shame and incalculable harm to the Evangelical Association and the cause of Christ. Only eternity can reveal the extent of the injury to priceless souls. Not only is the teaching of the Word of God plain and emphatic in reference to this matter, but our fathers also incorporated this law of the Word of God into our Discipline. A brief sentence only need be quoted:

"If any of our members shall enter a legal process against another member respecting any matter which might have been amically adjusted as above described, and before the measures hereby recommended are resorted to, they shall be excluded."

Our Discipline has not only made provision to settle financial difficulties arising between members, but also such as might arise between annual conferences and the incorporated societies of the church. On page 57, section 74, we have the following:

"The General Conference is the supreme court of law in the church; it shall decide upon the legality of all acts of annual conferences, and upon all such cases as may arise between any incorporated society of the church and its officers, and in its judicial capacity it shall decide, render verdict, and declare judgment only on such cases as are lawfully brought before it for adjudication."

From this it is obvious that if the Missionary Society or the Board of Publication, both of which are incorporated Societies, or the officers thereof, had deprived any individual or annual conference of their rights, they would have redress at the General Conference, the Supreme Court of law in the Church. However, A. M. Sampsel, W. E. Detweiler, George W. Brown, John Schneider, Benjamin C. Oyler, the Illinois Conference, the Platte River Conference, the Oregon Conference, and the Des Moines Conference, bring suit in the Court of Common Pleas of Cuyahoga County, in the State of Ohio, against J. J. Esher, Thomas Bowman, the Board of Publication, and the Missionary Society of the Evangelical Association! They do this not only before the General Conference, the Supreme Court of law in the church, can convene and make an attempt to adjust the differences if any exist; but even before these Societies can meet in their annual sessions and the claims of these parties, if any they had, could be passed upon. This act on their part was not only a clear violation of the Word of God, but also of our Discipline, which these parties vowed to defend and obey. Afterwards C.

S. Haman, W. F. Heil, and B. J. Smoyer united as accessories to the great crime, for which together with A. M. Sampsel they have been deposed from the office of the Christian ministry and expelled from the church. They have made the record for themselves before man and God. As it meets them to-day at every step and turn of life, so it will follow them through life, and meet them at the great Day. These parties and their associates in this great sin have been talking and writing about "arbitration," and yet they deliberately and wilfully trample under foot that sensible and equitable plan to arbitrate all difficulties, upon which the church had agreed, and adopted as a part of her constitution. They even appeal to Cæsar before they present their claims to the societies of the Church which they drag into the civil courts. It was a very cowardly piece of business on their part to prate about "arbitration" after they had carried their case into the courts, even before they presented their claims to the Church, and the Church had an opportunity to pass upon them. It was as silly as it was cowardly. To Cæsar they have appealed and Cæsar must now settle the affairs. It would be interesting to know how these arbitrations made by Cæsar thus far suit them. How confident in their mad frenzy they were of success. How bitterly they must be disappointed after spending tens of thousands of dollars wrested from their dupes in vain. For the useless waste of money and precious time, which might have been used to build up Christ's kingdom, for the animosities and ill feeling which has been engendered through these lawsuits, for the disgrace they have brought upon the cause of Christ in general, and upon our own Church particularly, and the loss of immortal souls, which have cost the blood of Christ, the leaders of this secession are responsible at the bar of God.

However, as above stated, the division of the Church had been decided upon so that these suits in Cleveland were part and parcel of the plan mapped out. Every one who took part in these procedings did it with the full knowledge that he was grossly violating the provisions of the Discipline of the Church, which he had promised to defend and obey, and knew that by this act he placed himself outside of the Church ; but having decided upon leaving the Church and setting up for themselves at some place to be decided upon in the future, they were utterly unconcerned as to the character of their conduct. No one took part in these proceedings except members of Annual Conferences where the seceders were in the majority, and having adopted a "business rule" requiring two-thirds of the conference to convict any one accused of crime, they felt perfectly safe in defying the law of the Church.

Such sad facts as have been portrayed in this volume could occur only in a Church which insists upon the necessity of experimental religion. Only men who were once enlightened and converted, but who again fall into sin, can be capable of pursuing such an unholy course. The Church, however is not without blame. The conduct of the leaders in this difficulty was known to many long before any disciplinary action was taken. It was a matter of common notoriety already during the first quadrennium of Bishop Dubs' episcopacy that he was in the habit of exaggeration and prevarication. Those who knew him best discounted his statements very largely, and were accustomed to ask themselves the question, "Is it true?" This was the case with his private and public statements, and more especially with the sensational stories related by him in his sermons, of which he was usually the hero. Many of the facts given in this volume were known to a good many long before any action was taken, besides the half dozen or more rumors seriously affecting his purity. No explanation was asked for or given except the instances referred to in this volume. Privately his attention was called to the rumors, yet he did nothing to stop their circulation. But at the General Conference in Allentown the friends of Bishop Dubs did all in their power to prevent an investigation of the serious allegations made against him by his colleagues. The strongest possible pressure was brought to bear upon the General Conference and upon Bishops Esher and Bowman to endeavor in some way to adjust the pending difficulties without instituting disciplinary proceedings and investigating the matter thoroughly.

Moreover, how long the Hartzlers were suffered; suffered long after it was known that they had willfully deceived the Church! Yea, endured a long while after they publicly antagonized the Church as she had given expression to her views through the Board of Missions, one of the most representative bodies of the Church in the interim of the General Conference. For months they were allowed to use the official organ of the Church to set at naught the authorities and antagonize the regulations it had made. In addition to this his personal conduct at the session of the Board of Missions in Cleveland, Ohio, in 1885, was outrageous. So also his wicked attempt at Indianapolis, Indiana, in 1886, to unduly influence the Board of Missions, fearing the results of an impartial investigation into affairs as reported by Bishop Esher, by circulating a pamphlet surreptitiously among such members of the Board with whom he considered his secret safe.—And Jacob Hartzler was allowed to remain in Japan long after his utter incompetency and faithlessness to the interests of the mission had been apparent. John Schneider and William Huelster were allowed to sit in the General Conference of our Church when their treachery and dishonesty were no secret. Even Rudolph Dubs declared to Rev. C. K. Fehr during the General Conference at Allentown in 1883 that it was a shame that such a corrupt and dishonest man as William Huelster was allowed to sit in the highest ecclesiastical body in our Church, and yet he walked arm in arm with this same Huelster in that city, and they have been bosom friends all through these difficulties! The difficulties in our Church have not been caused by "tyranny and despotism," nor "by centralization of power," but by a laxity of Discipline. Men who set at naught the Discipline of the Church, and who were guilty of untruth and treachery were allowed not only in our pulpits, but in the highest ecclesiastical bodies of our Church. For the sake of peace the evil was borne with until it threatened to destroy the Church. Only two persons of all the offenders up to 1887 had been ecclesiastically dealt with for their attacks upon the Bishops, the Board of Missions, etc., and these two were William Huelster and H. B. Hartzler. The first was declared *not guilty* of the charge of slander by the Illinois Conference, *still the Conference said he must recall his slanders and ask Bishop Esher's pardon.* Even this was doing pretty well considering that "the ring" managed adroitly to select the committee which investigated the charges. H. B. Hartzler was simply deposed from his office as editor! Yet the papers of the seceders have made an ado about the men who had been slain as if hundreds had been tried and expelled. *In 1887 the rebellion was inaugurated and organized and set in motion in Buffalo, New York.* Nothing which has occurred since can be pleaded as a justification for the revolt. Any measures which may have become necessary since then to subdue the rebellion must be judged from this stand-point, and can in no wise be pleaded as a justification of Dubs' rebellion against the Evangelical Association.

CHAPTER XII.

The Situation at Present and the Outlook for the Future.

In referring to the situation at the time this chapter is written, we will commence in the "far West," namely in the Oregon Conference including the States of Oregon and Washington. In these bounds the seceders can truthfully sing, "Not a foot of land do we possess," etc. The church is in possession of all her church buildings, and parsonages, and the seceders are out in the cold. They have indeed erected a small church building, but it stands upon leased ground. Moreover it seems the majority of their ministers have seceded from the "minority," so that they are a minority indeed and in truth. So far as the church is concerned their presence in Oregon is hardly known, and in Washington they have nothing at all. The courts in Oregon did quick work. The seceders are enjoined from pretending to be the Oregon Conference of the Evangelical Association, and have been *compelled* to adopt a distinctive name.

In the Platte River Conference two cases have been decided by the Courts. One has been decided in favor of the seceders which has been appealed, and will be heard by the Supreme Court in a few months. The other has been decided in favor of the church and no appeal was taken. This case included two churches and two parsonages which are now in undisputed possession of the church.

In the Des Moines Conference Judge Conrad has also decided a case involving three churches in Des Moines in favor of the church giving a clear and strong opinion. Judge Preston thereupon enjoined the seceders from holding an annual conference, or a quarterly conference. Hence they could make no appointments. Each preacher returned of his own accord to where he had been the previous year, hence as appointments in our church are made for one year only they have no ecclesiastical authority whatever. Several injunctions have since been obtained giving the church the use of her property. The Des Moines case will also be argued before the Supreme Court ere long, and when decided will settle matters in Iowa. The seceders illegally hold several churches belonging to the Iowa Conference, which cases will also be settled with the decision in the Des Moines case.

In Illinois the seceders have one solitary church left them. The Adams St. English Church in Chicago. This church they burdened with a debt of $12,000.00 to $14,000.00, and then allowed it to be sold at Sheriff's sale nearly 2 years ago, so that it is now owned by a private individual. The Sunday-school and the congregation have dwindled down to nearly nothing, and it is only a question of time when the church will be closed altogether. The Sheffield Avenue Church was for several years in possession of parties who have again seceded from the seceders and claim to be independent, but have recently surrendered the property to the Church. Their preacher was the Secretary of Dubs' General Conference in Philadelphia. No Dubs preacher has been allowed to preach in it as a regular pastor, and even Dubs himself was and is excluded. The seceders may have two or three thousand people scattered through the State, and will be able to build churches at various points.

However, aside from Barrington, Des Plaines, Naperville and the seceders from Noble St. in Chicago and a few other places, their congregations will be very weak and, I predict, will remain weak—in fact, grow less from year to year. The decision of the Supreme Court in favor of the Church, its refusal to grant a re-hearing, and the injunction issued by Judge Cartwright enjoining them from holding an Annual Conference in the name of the Church has settled matters finally in Illinois.

Coming eastward we next touch Ohio. Here the seceders fired their "big gun" at the Publishing House located in Cleveland. The gun, however, kicked very badly and hurt those who fired it worse than those it was aimed at. Then came the law suit of the seceders after their so-called General Conference in Philadelphia against the officers elected by the General Conference in Indianapolis to oust them from their positions by quo warranto proceedings. This gun, however, kicked worse than the first. The Circuit Court in a clear decision rendered by Judge Upson and his two associates, affirmed the title of the officers elected by the General Confereuce in Indianapolis, Ind. After a long delay the case was carried up to the Supreme Court. In order to have an early decision the church asked to have the case advanced, which has been granted, and was set for a hearing in November. The seceders strenuously opposed the advancement of the hearing, fearing no doubt that the decision of the Supreme Court will also be adverse. The arguments on both sides were filed in printed briefs before Jan. 1, 1894. After the decision of the Supreme Court of Ohio has been rendered *somebody* will be compelled to raise a considerable amount of money to pay the tremendous costs involved in the hearing of those cases. The officers of the church have not yet felt any necessity to make preparation to pay the enormous bill. Then, as we confidently believe the decision will be in our favor, the few churches which the seceders now have in their possession in this State will also revert to the church. Perhaps nowhere have the ministers who have sided with the revolt acted in a more despicable manner than the few who have turned traitors to the Ohio Conference. They professed loyalty to the church, accepted appointments from both Bishops Esher and Bowman, one was even ordained by Bishop Bowman after the proceedings had against him in Chicago, and the same man even at the last session previous to the General Conference of 1891 signed the proceedings as a token of acquiescence and obedience, par-

held a secret conclave and "elected delegates to Philadelphia!" Benedict Arnold was a gentleman compared with such treasonable individuals. Of course a cause in the hands of such glaringly dishonest men cannot and will not succeed. Their "conference" will grow less and less until it becomes extinct.

Next comes Pennsylvania. This is at present the real battle ground between the contending forces. For reasons of their own the litigation committee has not yet very vigorously pushed things in the bounds of the Central Pa. and Pittsburgh Conferences, preferring to fight the matter out in the East Pa. Conference although several cases have now also been commenced in the Central Pa. and Pittsburgh Conferences. Here a number of cases are pending. Equity cases in Pennsylvania are always slow, and it seems cases of this kind especially so. The language used by the writer in his opening address at the last General Conference on this point has been abundantly verified. Speaking of these things he said: "They have staked their all in the warfare in which they have engaged. Hence we must be prepared, not only for war, but also for occasional reverses; yea, even for dark, trying hours and days, and perhaps years. Legal processes at the best are tedious, uncertain, and often provoking." Let this language be compared with our experience in our litigation in general, and it will be seen how correct it is.

Judge Endlich, of Reading, Pa., decided against the General Conference at Indianapolis. What he decided about the Philadelphia body is of no importance in the case. Even he could not find that body to have any ecclesiastical jurisdiction. His opinion, should it be sustained, would disorganize the Evangelical Association. The pieces could be gathered by whomsoever might be able to find them. However, in view of the decision already rendered by the Supreme Court of Pennsylvania in the Bangor case in which it is clearly stated that the decisions of the highest ecclesiastical court are binding upon the civil courts, there is no danger that Judge Endlich's decision will be allowed to stand. Moreover, the Supreme Court of Pennsylvania has taken exactly the same position in reference to the questions which have arisen in the U. B. Church. How can the court, having rendered such decisions, "go behind the returns" in reference to the proceedings of the General Conference at Buffalo, N. Y. ? Any other course would revolutionize all ecclesiastical proceedings and take away the right of self-government from the Churches. It will never be done.

Since Judge Endlich's decision Master J. W. Wood, of Allentown, Pa., has filed an opinion, involving three churches, strongly and clearly in favor of the Church. This case was argued before Judge Albright, of Lehigh Co., in October. Recently also, Master Stewart of Easton, has reported in favor of the Church, in the case of the St. John's Church, Bethlehem. We expect that the cases will come before the Supreme Court in February or March next, and we will have a decision by June or July of 1894. Hence we will need to exercise patience probably for a year longer. By that time the hope is entertained this vexed question will be settled in Iowa, Nebraska, Ohio and Pennsylvania, as it has been settled in Oregon and Illinois, so that when the next General Conference meets in Elgin, Illinois, all litigation will be ended, and all the energies of the Church can again be devoted to building up the interests of our Zion and in the salvation of souls.

THE OUTLOOK.

We will again commence in the "far West." In Oregon at the time the conference was divided by the treason of J. Bowersox, there were but five brethren in the active work who remained loyal to the Church, namely H. Shuknecht, H. I. Bittner, Peter Bittner, I. B. Fisher and L. S. Fisher. The brethren N. Shupp and J. E. Stoops had been sent to the Coast during the previous year, but were not yet conference members. The brethren M. Burlingname, J. M. Preiss, J. Erich, A. Ernst and G. M. McElroy, local ministers, also stood firm and were received and given appointments, and a young brother, H. E. Weber, from Spokane, was also put to work. So that after all we could put thirteen ministers into the field at the first session of the regenerated conference. The number since 1890 has increased to twenty-seven in active work, with five or six active local preachers. It is indeed the Lord's doing. Well may we exclaim, "What hath God wrought?" Moreover, the conference is saved from an incubus which has hindered its growth and prosperity. At no time had our Church such an outlook for future growth and usefulness on the Pacific Coast as it has at this time if the brethren in the ministry remain true to themselves, to the Church and true to Christ.

In the Des Moines Conference Kooker and Utt had tyrannized over the young men to such a degree that but six out of some fifty preachers remained loyal, namely J. H. Yaggy. J. F. Yerger, S. W. Kiplinger, J. Wirth, L. N. Day and G. F. Heilman. Four or five local preachers also remained true. Soon afterwards, however, the brethren J. McCurdy and J. McCauley returned to the fold with their charges. As it had been made almost a condition of membership in this conference to root the *Evangelical Messenger* out of our families and introduce the seceders' organ, the people became very much embittered and the conflict has been severe. However, thus far the Church has gained all along the line. While the gain has not been as large comparatively on the Pacific Coast, still the increase has been encouraging. The conference has increased from six to seventeen active men in the field. It is confidently believed that if the Supreme Court of the State affirms Judge Conrad's decision, of which there is little doubt, that hundreds of our members will remain with the Church. Upon the whole the societies in the Des Moines Conference are not very strong numerically, and at but few places will the seceders either be willing or able to build new churches simply to give the disloyal ministers an opportunity to earn their bread. All they need do is to accept the ministers the legal Des Moines Conference sends them and they can worship in the churches unmolested. Why go and build new churches?

In the Platte River Conference when "it stepped down and out" at the behest of a few dishonest and ignorant leaders, the conference being composed almost exclusively of young men, only one brother in the active work, namely Bro. J. P. Ash, stood loyal for his Church, and in order to make things solid for the seceders they called a "trial committee" and attempted to silence him. However, they did not succeed very well. Their proceedings were set aside by the courts and Bro. Ash vindicated from the persecutions of a set of graceless and wicked men. Several local elders, namely Bro. M. L. Custer and S. W. McKesson also remained loyal. The conference was re-organized in the Spring of 1891, and now counts seven members, about as many as there were when the conference was first organized. It will take hard and patient work to recover the lost ground. A great deal of the labor and money expended will be lost. C. W. Anthony and A. W. Shenberger could not have so completely ruined this conference had not E. L. Kiplinger come upon the scene, backed by the influence and the money of the Einsel's— at least as long as they were in accord and their money lasted. After they will be compelled to turn over the property of the Church probably after all a good many of the people may remain. In this conference, as in Oregon, many of the seceders have seceded from the secession and gone elsewhere.

In Illinois the Lord has done great things for those who have remained faithful. Nowhere perhaps did the rebellion present a bolder front than here—nowhere perhaps were the loyal ministers and people treated with as much contempt, and nowhere perhaps was the evil spirit which characterized the movement at all places, so fearfully evil as in this State. Nowhere were the leaders of the movement so corrupt and utterly without conscience as here, and nowhere were the ministers in general who went with the movement so graceless as in Illinois. Then, too, the presence of their chief, Rudolph Dubs, who after his suspension as bishop and minister moved to Chicago and became editor of the German organ of the faction inflamed the opposition all the more. Into this paper Dubs poured all the malignity and ugliness of which he was capable, doing his utmost to embitter his followers against the Church and all connected with it. Hence the victory achieved is all the grander and greater. Fully three-fourths of our membership will be saved for the Church, and it will be a much more spiritual conference than it was for years. The best elements among our membership having remained loyal to our Church, and the better portion of those who, under the influence of the seceding ministers, were led away, it is hoped will see their error and return to the fold. For the last fifteen or twenty years the leaders were entirely unconcerned about the spiritual welfare of themselves or the people. They were running things "for revenue only," with the addition of securing ecclesiastical power. Those even who remained loyal to the spirit of our Church and true to its doctrine and genius were made the subjects of persecution and were completely terrorized by the leaders.

Of the large conference only the following remained faithful and true when "the ring" closed the Church against Bishop Esher at Sheffield Avenue: C. Augenstein, J. Alber, C. Danner, J. B. Elfrink, A. Egli, E. v. Freeden, D. E. Fehr, W. Goessele, C. Hummel, J. G. Kleinknecht, J. C. Kiest, H. A. Kramer, J. J. Lintner, W. Neitz, F. C. Neitz, C. Ott, H. Pope, W. Schmus, C. Schmucker, F. Schwartz, W. A. Schultz, G. Vetter, C. Vaubel, L. Willman, A. Woehr, J. Wellner and J. Zipperer. These had been in the active work. Besides these there were a number of other ministers who were in the itinerancy but not in active service, among whom were the venerable Henry Bucks, J. Lutz, H. Rotermund, E. Musselman, J. C. Spielman and others, besides some local ministers who remained faithful. Then of those employed in the college at Naperville, President A. A. Smith, since gone to glory, J. Lerch and Prof. Kletzing stood firm and true. Twenty-five were left who could take work in the distracted conference, while the seceders had probably sixty-five. *The twenty-five have now grown* to sixty-five, who are at work in this conference to-day in the short span of three years! All of them have as much, and some of them more than they can do, and every one getting full support, and a nice surplus left in the missionary treasury, while the former puffed-up followers of Dubs are dwindled down to one-half of their former proportions without a church or parsonage they can truthfully call their own. The churches they are now building are all independent of any ecclesiastical organization. The "regulars" in Illinois are altogether "without form and void." In a few years our work in the boundaries of this conference will have fully recovered from the ravages Dubsism had made upon it.

In the East Pennsylvania Conference the brethren claim at least seven thousand who have not bowed their knees to the Baal of secession, and should the Supreme Court of the State, (of which the writer does not entertain a particle of doubt), decide in favor of the Church, it is expected that the majority of our membership will remain with the Church, which has been instrumental in their salvation. Within the boundaries of this conference, and in fact throughout Pennsylvania, the seceders have largely succeeded in carrying the people with them by arousing their prejudices against the European element in our Church. They raised the cry, "The Germans want to rule us," and "The Germans do rule us," meaning thereby the European element, they mostly also speaking German, although they belong to the oldest settlers of the country. It seems strange that such a cry should be successful in view of the fact that Dubs' allies in Illinois and those who seceded from, as well as those who were expelled, by the Iowa Conference were nearly all Europeans.

Moreover no pains were spared to prejudice the laity against the authorities of the Church, and whereas the soil had been well prepared for years by inveighing against "the Cleveland ring" and "the Germans out there," it was a comparatively easy task to inflame the passions and arouse the prejudices of the people. Even the family relations of the bishops were not spared, but made to do service in the cause of destruction.

At the Annual Conference at Shamokin, Pa., in 1890, the meanness and bitterness of the leaders of secession, could be seen and felt in all its ugliness. Every movement they made, every election that was held, had but one purpose in view, namely to strengthen the position and forces of rebeldom. Bishop Esher found on meeting with the presiding elders to make the appointments that the intention was if possible to make the same in such a way as to crush out every sentiment of loyalty among the ministry and the people. And finding that he was not sufficiently acquainted with affairs to counteract their plans, he wired for his colleague who was in bed suffering all the distress of la grippe. The writer however replied, "Hold the fort till I come," and almost at the peril of his life came to the help of his colleague. While it was impossible to make the appointments fully satisfactory so as to save the loyal congregations, nevertheless the plans of the disloyal set of elders were frustrated to a large extent, and much injury and loss averted. And while the bishops finally consented to make a change in one instance, from the program they had adopted, and consented to this because they were convinced it would be for the best ultimately, C. S. Haman went into court in Hastings, Neb., and solemnly swore the appointments were made as the presiding elders wanted them. But this was not the only thing he swore to there which was not true, it is to be hoped on account of his stupidity and lack of mental vigor to know what he is about.

The appointments made at Shamokin, Pa., in 1890, made the appointments of 1891 in Allentown, Pa., possible. The secessionists had been predicting "Bishop Bowman will have ten preachers to stand by him, and two charges to which to send them." However, thank God, their prophecies greatly failed,

failed in spite of the secret meeting the conspirators held in Reading, Pa., to take steps to prevent Bishop Bowman from presiding at the conference at Allentown, Pa. There it was agreed to unite the laymen and congregations against the authorities of the Church, and a form of resolutions to be presented to the Quarterly Conferences was agreed upon, and so the conspiracy be finally completed. And yet, notwithstanding all these efforts there was a respectable number of ministers who refused to bow their necks to the yoke which Dubs and Company so effectually and securely placed upon the necks of the majority of the conference. The names of those who were willing to "stand up and be counted" for loyalty to the Church against all the storm of persecution raised around them are herewith given in alphabetical order:

Breyfogel S. C., Bohner B. F., Bliem J. C., Brown S. B., Bowman James, Bartholomew D., Dreher C. D., Ely S., Fehr C. K., Fehr J. K., Fredericks W. E., Gingrich C., Goebel N., Gruver P. A., Hess I., Hoffman F., Harper Thomas, Heisler I. F., Krecker A., Knobel G. C., Krupp B. C., Kindt A., Kresge A. S., Leopold W. A., Leopold S. T., Lentz David, Manning D. S., Newhart J. C., Reineck W. H., Specht Joseph, Saylor O. L., Stauffer W. H., Wieand W. K., Weidner W. H., Williams A. E., Wentz Thomas L., Werner J. L., Zern J.

Besides these just named, some of whom could not take work on account of age and the condition of their health, the Lord sent us some very excellent young men, who were sent out on the field, so that instead of having "ten preachers and two fields," forty ministers were sent out, and this number has since increased to fifty-four appointed at the last conference session in Reading.

While it will take years of hard self-sacrificing work to repair the ruin that has been wrought, still after our people can again worship in their churches, now illegally held by the seceders, things will adjust themselves. The spirit among the ministers and people is that of great hope and God is with them.

At the Central and Pittsburg Conferences there were so few loyal ministers left that no conference sessions could be held until after the session of General Conference in the Spring of 1892. Then these conferences were again organized. In the Central but seven or eight could be appointed. Here the work of destruction has reached the highest point of any locality in the Church, and yet there are hundreds of members throughout the conference territory, who are still loyal to the Church, and no doubt thousands will remain with the fold when the disloyal ministers must once vacate the pulpits, which will happen ere long. In the Pittsburg Conference twelve men have been appointed, and as in the Central no doubt many will remain with the Church when once the property question is settled.

Thus, has been written perhaps one of the saddest histories connected with any church difficulty of modern times. There was absolutely no cause for it, but the unholy ambition of men determined to rule or ruin. The ruin so far as numbers are concerned, under the blessing of God, is not as great as they had confidently expected. In their blind zeal they had counted on sixty to seventy thousand of our members to go with them. The writer of this volume again ventures to assert that when the next General Conference meets in Elgin, Ill., and by that time our statistics can again be correctly given, it will be found that the loss in membership will not exceed 30,000.

The institutions of the Church, notwithstanding these difficulties are in a flourishing condition. Although the expenses for litigation are enormous, the finances of our Publishing House are not very much different from what they usually are. The subscription lists are nearly up to the old figures before the trouble commenced. The Missionary Society has not curtailed its operations, but in some instances has increased them. The income from "Children's Day" this year has been larger than on any previous occasion. Moreover, a special effort is being made which will no doubt largely decrease the old missionary indebtedness.

The Orphan Home, located at Flat Rock, O., has been very much enlarged at a heavy expense in the midst of all these troubles, and more acreage secured, and all paid for, so that we now have at least one-fourth more children in the home than at any previous time, and money in the treasury. An "Old People's Home" has been organized, valuable property secured, and paid for, in the city of Philadelphia, by members of our Church in that city, also all done since these troubles are going on.

So also in Germany a Deaconesses Home has been founded at a great expense, and some seventy deaconesses trained and put to work at various places on the continent, right in the throes through which the Church has passed.

Our senior Bishop has just returned from Japan, where he has organized the Japan Conference, under the signal blessings of God, with nearly twenty native ministers, and five American missionaries. Thus have we been going forward in the Name of the Lord, and our hearts are big with hope for the future of the Evangelical Association, provided she retains sound doctrine and strict Discipline.

"The best of all is, God is with us."

www.ingramcontent.com/pod-product-compliance
Lightning Source LLC
Chambersburg PA
CBHW021842230426
43669CB00008B/1051